ESSENTIAL
PSYCHOLOGY

General Editor
Peter Herriot

C4

CULTURE'S INFLUENCE ON
BEHAVIOUR

ESSENTIAL

PSYCHOLOGY

CULTURE'S INFLUENCE ON BEHAVIOUR

Robert Serpell

Methuen

First published 1976 by Methuen & Co Ltd
11 New Fetter Lane, London EC4P 4EE
© 1976 Robert Serpell
Printed in Great Britain by
Richard Clay (The Chaucer Press), Ltd
Bungay, Suffolk

ISBN (hardback) 0 416 82240 1
ISBN (paperback) 0 416 82250 9

We are grateful to Grant McIntyre of
Open Books Publishing Ltd
for assistance in the preparation of this series

Contents

Acknowledgements

This book was written at one fell swoop, so that regrettably I was not able to ask any colleagues to comment on it in draft form. Since, however, many of the views it presents have been tried out and modified in discussion, I should like to acknowledge a special debt for their willingness to discuss, to Jan Deregowski and Phil Kingsley. The critical interest shown by students at the University of Zambia has also been a great encouragement. For typing of the manuscript I am indebted to Steven Chikakuda, Suwilanji Kalolo and Ilse Mwanza. Peter Herriot and Namposhya Serpell read the first draft and helped me see what to leave out, and what was unclear. What remains is, of course, my own responsibility.

I am grateful to Dr William Hudson and the editors of *The Journal of Social Psychology* and *Psychologia Africana* for permission to re-produce figures 6.1 and 6.6.

Editor's Introduction

Psychologists confidently make statements about people in general from their observations and experiments. But how justified are we in doing so? Perhaps our theories relate only to Western industrial man. Robert Serpell discusses in this book such general questions as how different cultures relate to the personality of their members, and such specific ones as the extent to which people from different cultures are taken in by visual illusions. He leaves us with the uncomfortable suspicion that our psychological theories and methods are in turn the product of our own culture, and hence are inappropriate in the analysis of the culture and behaviour of others.

This book belongs to Unit C of *Essential Psychology*. What unifies the titles in this unit is the concept of development. It is a very rich concept, embodying as it does the notions of process and change, and the interaction of a human being with his environment throughout his life. The individual has to maintain some sort of equilibrium between the demands of the environment and his own way of constructing reality. He has to adapt to the realities of the particular culture he lives in; but at the same time, he may be able to change his environment to a certain extent. In this way, equilibrium may be maintained without compromising his own conceptual system. The concept of development is thus ideal for dealing with growing up and changing in society. We can use the phrase 'personal development' to talk both about children and about adults; this may help us to see both as people. The reader will find other conceptual frameworks in other units. They are not so much mutually contradictory as efforts to do justice to the complexities of psychology's subject matter. Coming to terms with a variety of explanatory frameworks decreases our confidence in psychology as a mature science; but perhaps it is better to be honest about what we don't know.

Essential Psychology as a whole is designed to reflect the changing structure and function of psychology. The authors are both academics and professionals, and their aim has been to introduce the most important concepts in their areas to beginning students. They have tried to do so clearly but have not attempted to conceal the fact that concepts that now appear central to their work may soon be peripheral. In other words, they have presented psychology as a developing set of views of man, not as a body of received truth. Readers are not intended to study the whole series in order to 'master the basics'. Rather, since different people may wish to use different theoretical frameworks for their own purposes, the series has been designed so that each title stands on its own. But it is possible that if the reader has read no psychology before, he will enjoy individual books more if he has read the introductions (A1, B1, etc.) to the units to which they belong. Readers of the units concerned with applications of psychology (E, F) may benefit from reading all the introductions.

A word about references in the text to the work of other writers – e.g. 'Smith, 1974'. These occur where the author feels he must acknowledge an important concept or some crucial evidence by name. The book or article referred to will be listed in the References (which double as Name Index) at the back of the book. The reader is invited to consult these sources if he wishes to explore topics further.

We hope you enjoy psychology.

Peter Herriot

I
Why cross-cultural psychology?

Every year one or two new academic journals are launched focusing on new areas of specialization. The main kind of justification which their editors offer is *de facto* recognition for a growing body of research. Although the immediate need to draw together a scattered range of material is real enough, I would like to suggest here some longer-term reasons for taking notice specifically of cross-cultural psychology:

(1) Contact between different cultures has assumed such proportions in the twentieth century that instead of asking 'why are other people so different from us?' we find observers increasingly wondering to what extent distinctive ways of life are likely to survive. 'Being different' in psychology includes holding different values. So the issue of how much diversity is to remain in the world concerns more than the tourist industry: it raises questions about morality. I believe that this aspect of political philosophy is not just an 'armchair' problem to be talked about after dinner. We need factual information and theoretical explanations about differences in values among the peoples of the world, some of which fall within the purview of cross-cultural psychology.

(2) If we can observe variations in culture by moving across the surface of the world, we can also do so by staying in one place and recording changes over time. Social change in the third world has greatly accelerated since 1950 and is compounded with culture contact. Many new states have imported wholesale features of 'Western' technology in an attempt to accelerate economic development. Large numbers of people

in these societies face particular problems of adaptation to this foreign culture's technology. This is the area of application for cross-cultural psychology whose significance has been most widely recognized.

(3) Psychological theory also stands to gain in its own right from the cross-cultural perspective. The aim of Watson's (1925) Behaviourism, to construct a set of universal laws applicable to all behaviour, has already been toned down by comparative studies of animals showing how different species have adapted their behaviour to fit their environment. Far too much of human psychology is based on studies of White Male Middle-Class Anglo-Saxon Protestant Undergraduates for us to attach much confidence to the claim that the models it generates describe general characteristics of human beings (see A3 of *Essential Psychology*).

1 *Political philosophy*

There are two very different lines of argument used to justify the equality of human rights. The '*sameness*' argument, very crudely, states that all people are basically the same: the differences among them are superficial and not worth taking seriously. Some individuals have not been given the opportunities offered to others to reach fulfilment of their potential. In an ideal world everyone would have the same opportunities and everyone would reach the same maximum level of fulfilment. The main difficulty with this view is that our definition of fulfilment tends to reflect a specific set of cultural values. For instance the degree of privacy cherished by middle-class English society would be viewed as intolerably lonely in many other communities. One man's fulfilment is another man's misfortune. In our search for ways of reducing prejudice and hostility between groups it is tempting to emphasize the similarities between them, and there is no doubt that these exist. But when we have drawn attention to the living humanity of all peoples and dispelled the clouds of misinformation, we are left with numerous instances of deeply cherished values in a given society which are genuinely distasteful to members of other groups.

The '*different but equal*' argument meets this problem by suggesting that each cultural group should specify its own set of objectives and be given equal opportunity to attain its chosen ideals. This view, however, raises different problems.

Many of the ingredients for one man's fulfilment involve the lives of other individuals. Cultures which in the past were widely separated geographically now coexist cheek by jowl in most of the world's big cities. Whole nations are in some cases built on the assumption of cooperation between two or more distinct ethnic groups. Not only individuals, but the groups themselves, are forced by the nature of the modern world to take account of each other's different values. The same need arises in the relations between successive generations of societies which are undergoing rapid social change.

A strong case can also be made that consciousness of alternatives is a fundamental right, without which the 'freedom' to fulfil oneself according to the lights of one's culture is illusory. To safeguard the values of a traditionally isolated rural community, if taken literally, would in many cases mean to deny the members of that society the opportunity of even a partial appreciation of the alternatives offered by a modern, technological, urban life. Many governments in Africa, Asia and South America now face the moral dilemma posed by growing shanty-towns where large numbers of people, attracted by the bright lights of the city, sample what they can of the new way of life, while the rural communities of their childhood are deprived of their chance of fulfilment by an exodus of working-age manpower. The shanty-town communities probably do not offer these 'immigrants' a fulfilling life by the standards of either culture; increasingly the rural communities cannot meet the ideals of the younger generation. There is no going back into mutual isolation from this situation. Both societies have to adapt, and in so doing to choose or compromise between the contradictory values of the diverse cultures from which they are growing.

This process of adaptation has been discussed under various headings: acculturation, urbanization and modernization are the most commonly used. Two of these terms explicitly emphasize one direction of change at the expense of the other, and the potentially ambiguous term, acculturation, is in practice used almost invariably to refer to Westernization, i.e. the same direction. Moreover all three terms suggest that the individual is merely acted on by his environment. If we start from the assumption that any two cultures have equal moral validity, then there is no simple moral reason to suppose that most (let alone all) of the changes should be on one side. Progress, whether for an individual or for a society, means not passive assimilation by an imposed system

11

with its own values but active choice among alternatives with the object of achieving one's own ideals.

The study of cultures in contact has been approached from a great variety of perspectives and disciplines. Social anthropologists have studied in the new cities of the third world the complex interaction between traditional customs and beliefs and the demands of industrial employment and urban residence. Political scientists have analysed how the interests of members of different groups can coincide in certain types of interaction and the ways in which economically powerful colonizers have manipulated this situation to their advantage. Literary commentators have described the emotional strains which those without power must endure in dual societies which teach all their members to aspire to certain goals but reserve the right to attain them for members of the oppressor group. Yet in all this literature we lack a systematic comparison of the alternative values held by the groups which are interacting and how they relate to survival and success in a given social setting.

One psychological line of enquiry has been to survey the attitudes of various groups of people who occupy intermediate positions between cultures, such as teachers in developing countries, who have passed through a local, traditional social upbringing and an imported, Western formal education. What compromise have these people struck, which of the values characteristic of the same profession in other cultures do they share, and which are more closely associated with the traditions of their homes? Another dimension of how different cultures interact is suggested by the study of mental illness in the context of social change. Analysis of the origins of such illness may reveal certain patterns of response to conflicting values which are demonstrably unsuccessful. The identification of a person as mentally ill, however, is never a straightforward task (see F1), and it becomes additionally complex when clinical practice is only dimly related to society's criteria. Behaviour which is intolerable in one community may be quite acceptable in another. Thus before we can approach the question of what social conditions precipitate mental disorder, we are faced with a very difficult problem of assessment.

2 Social change

Although we may consider on a philosophical plane that moral values have meaning only in relation to a particular culture, governments in the modern world operate as if they are appealing to moral values without specifying their cultural context. The concepts of progress and development are used to justify policies for social change without explaining in detail how they relate to the existing values of particular communities. The predominant criteria are economic and are presumably related to the universal human desires for food, shelter and protection from disease. But the great majority of development programmes choose a highly specific way of meeting these needs. Their standard 'solution' to the problem includes cities with a cash economy, mechanical industries, large housing estates, motorized transport, formal schooling with an emphasis on literacy, on numeracy and on Western science, Western medical facilities, and Western amenities for entertainment.

The individual who wishes to partake of the fruits of development is thus presented with a package which interprets 'the good life' in a highly specific way. If he is to prosper in this 'modern' environment he must know how to use its facilities. Even if we assume that he has adopted the basic goals of the urban culture, there are many other respects in which an upbringing in a non-Western, rural environment constitutes an inappropriate preparation for city life. The importance of the adjustments called for can be viewed from two angles, that of the society's group goals such as economic productivity, or that of the individual's personal goals such as avoiding painful accidents. Most observers would agree that the two are to a large extent interdependent, although they can clearly diverge in specific instances.

Psychological research has investigated this discrepancy between the requirements of urban life and the behaviour of 'unacculturated' people along several dimensions. The usual strategy has been to simulate a feature of the urban environment within a test situation and to compare performance on the test by groups of people from different cultural backgrounds. In this way it has been demonstrated within the limits of the experimental conditions that 'unacculturated' groups, relative to Western-educated groups, show different and often lower task motivation, a less analytic style of thought, less abstract and less logical interpretation of the test materials and procedures, and less comprehension of specific conventions of pictorial representation.

Each of these dimensions is defined and measured in terms of a particular theoretical view developed in the first place to explain the behaviour of Western-educated people. In trying

13

to interpret the cross-cultural differences in performance on the tests we have therefore to disentangle problems of definition and measurement from the search for causal accounts of how the cultural environment affects the development of attitudes and skills. If these methodological problems can be solved, it may be possible to derive from this research some practical suggestions for overcoming the difficulty of adjustment faced by large numbers of people caught up in the rapidly expanding trend of world urbanization and industrialization. Suggestions which have already been proposed range over a wide area of social action, from specific training techniques in industry and general education methods in schools, to pre-school facilities and child-rearing methods in the home.

A more immediate application of psychology to the problem posed by the mismatch between the skills and attitudes generally present in the population of third world countries and the demands of industrial tasks in their cities is the design of selection procedures. Competition is normally very high in these countries for jobs in industry because of the relatively high economic benefits they offer. Employers therefore increasingly look for ways of basing their inevitably limited selection on criteria which will predict successful adjustment by the employee to the requirements of his job. Although there is no need to look beyond the motive of maximizing profit to explain the employer's concern in this regard, it is arguable that the whole industrial community benefits from job satisfaction which is presumably enhanced by successful adjustment. The very extensive literature on selection test development will not however receive much attention in this book. The pragmatic orientation of researchers in this field has tended to leave little room for trying to separate the measurement of general adaptability from that of adaptation to the specific dictates of Western technological culture.

3 Psychological theory

The study of mind has posed such an intractable problem for the methods of objective science that many psychologists agreed at the beginning of this century to reformulate the scope of their enquiry as the science of behaviour (see A1). This brought within the realm of psychology the study of animals other than man. The early studies with dogs, pigeons and (above all) rats are well known (see A3). The objective

14

of deriving laws of behaviour which would explain learning and other processes across all species has been qualified in several ways under the impact of new theories. The science of ethology, the study of species-specific behaviour (see D2), has drawn attention to the naïveté of taking as a representative sample of behaviour the responses made, under severe deprivation and in an artificially restricted environment, by animals raised in cages from birth. The particular adaptations by different species to their habitat have begun to be studied in the field and will eventually provide an elaborate framework for understanding the differences across species in response to particular psychological tests (Eibl-Eibesfeldt, 1970).

Meanwhile the evolutionary perspective emphasized by ethology has been brought to bear on mankind. The notion of man's uniqueness, which was discounted by the early Behaviourists, has been revived in the context of language, which seems to be a peculiarly human adaptation (see Lenneberg, 1967). Here it has been recognized that the internal properties of language need to be considered in their own right in trying to explain the psychological processes involved, rather than simply subsuming language under the broad headings of perception, response and learning (see A7). Alongside the growth of psycholinguistics, there has been a revival of interest in other cognitive processes such as decision, planning and reasoning. The complexity of these processes has drawn attention to the contrast not only between man and other animals but also between adult and infant humans. The amazing vulnerability and ineptitude of the human neonate is interpreted as a by-product of the extreme plasticity of the human brain which permits the most elaborate and specialized adaptations by means of learning.

Yet, despite the realization that the behaviour of a species can only be properly understood in the context of the environment to which evolution has adapted it, and that man's adaptation includes a primary emphasis on learning during the individual's life time, there has been little attempt in psychology to relate man's behaviour to the full range of environments he encounters. The great majority of studies of any psychological process in man have been confined to the most readily available human subjects at the centres of research, i.e. the students at Western universities. Replication of the occasional experiment with servicemen or industrial workers has by and large confirmed the results, generating an unwarranted confidence in the generality of the theories which have been proposed. Studies of child development and of ageing

15

have not been seen as a threat to this generality since the processes of biological maturation and decay can conveniently explain away the gross differences in behaviour which are observed. Even sex differences, class differences and individual differences in behaviour when they are observed have often been attributed to genetic factors.

Aside from a few isolated studies, virtually no attempt was made until the 1960s to look at variations in behaviour across the wide range of cultural environments represented around the world. There seem to be two prevalent assumptions among psychologists about the great majority of the world's population: either (1) they are essentially the same as the Western population which contributed the subjects for the existing body of human psychological research; or (2) they are so different from the Western population that they are best considered an abnormal group to be reserved for specialized study. Assumption (1) becomes extremely implausible if we consider the existing evidence from the West on sex differences and social class differences in behaviour. If the comparatively minor variations in environment within the Western world associated with the sub-cultures of sex and class can be shown to exercise a reliable influence on behaviour, we can reasonably expect to find at least as great and reliable differences in behaviour when we compare Western subjects to people from radically different cultures.

The other extreme, assumption (2), would scarcely deserve mention, were it not so apparent in the informal reactions of many psychologists to the field of cross-cultural psychology. Suffice it to point out that a science of behaviour which can account only for the behaviour of a minority of the world's population is far more appropriately designated a limited speciality than the search for explanations which account for the full range of human behaviour patterns around the world. Cross-cultural psychology is still a long way from permitting a reasonable answer to the question of whether most human behaviour is independent of the influence of culture or the balance is on the other side. But it seems beyond question that cultural variations in behaviour are an essential subject of study in psychology for the validation of many generalizations about human behaviour, which are presently based on a very narrowly restricted sample of the world's population.

Most cross-cultural studies are concerned to establish a causal link between variations in the cultural environment and variations in behaviour. This should be clearly distinguished from comparisons on the basis of race or colour in which the causal link sought is between genetic or constitutional factors and behaviour. Thus cross-cultural psychology, as contrasted with cross-racial psychology, is designed to generate theoretical explanations in the environmentalist (or empiricist) tradition. In practice, very few cross-cultural studies have made any serious attempt to control genetic factors across the cultural groups which they compare. But the focus of interest is on environmental determinants of behaviour so that the great majority of explanations offered in these studies assume that the behaviour under discussion has been learned. The validity of this assumption can, of course, be debated, but I shall not do so in this book (see D4).

The range of psychological constructs which have been examined in this way include motivation and cognition. Culture has been conceived as affecting motivation at the level of the total personality, of attitudes and of specific motives; it has been conceived as affecting cognition at the level of the broad structure of intellect and of specific processes such as reasoning, communication and perception. Aspects of culture which might exercise such an influence include social and physical characteristics of the environment. Evidently cultures vary in the norms of interpersonal behaviour which they specify, a particularly striking example being language. They also offer different ranges of occupational specialities which provide for characteristic social and physical learning conditions. The physical environment of the whole community is also structured by culture in terms of the style of its artefacts and its general impact on the community's habitat.

As Fig. 1.1 suggests, there is no reason to suppose that the physical and social environment are independent of each other, nor that motivation and cognition are independent. Nevertheless most of the theorizing in cross-cultural psychological research is concerned with specifying the details of causal relationships within the general scope of the solid lines in Fig. 1.1. The research designs typically record variations in behaviour as a function of variations in culture, so that the theories are based on a very indirect assessment of evidence.

An additional complication in this already daunting array of interacting factors is that an individual's personality and intellect will clearly influence the way in which he learns from his environment. We can thus postulate a cumulative learning process over the individual's lifetime in which his motivational and cognitive processes are initially structured by the cultural environment and subsequently determine what he will continue to learn from that environment. In this sense any cross-cultural theory in psychology must include a developmental perspective. Many of the explanations we will consider in the following chapters are explicitly related to theories of child development. The remainder tend to emphasize the early years of life as the most critical for the impact of culture on psychological processes.

Because the range of behaviour susceptible to cultural influence is so wide, a variety of different classifications can be

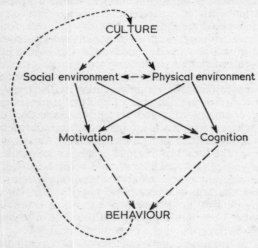

Fig. 1.1 *Some of the causal relationships mediating the relation between culture and behaviour*

suggested for research in this field. The approach I have adopted in this book is to concentrate on a number of specific theoretical issues which have dominated research in the past twenty years. Each of these issues arises from a combination of different concerns, some central to the impact of culture on behaviour, others suggested by Western psychological theory or by practical applications of psychological methods. The facet of the discipline which links these various concerns is as broad as the facets described as physiological psychology (see A2) and comparative psychology. Cross-cultural psychology, like these other fields, views the whole gamut of psychological processes (perception, learning, memory, thought, intelligence, skill, communication, motivation, emotion, personality) from a particular perspective. Just as the relation between mind and body dominates the problems of physiological psychology, we will find certain recurrent problems dominating cross-cultural research on different psychological processes. In Chapter 7 I shall attempt to draw these together in a discussion of methodology. The difficulties, I shall suggest, arise not so much from a lack of technical refinements, but rather from very basic conceptual features of the attempt by man to look objectively at cultures of which he lacks a first-hand, 'insider's' experience.

The organization of the remaining chapters proceeds from the more general to the more specific, starting with the global approach of anthropological, culture-and-personality theory (Ch. 2) and ending with the highly specialized topic of cross-cultural differences in the perception of pictures (Ch. 6). The main emphasis of the book is on cognitive and perceptual processes, reflecting my own interests. In this field the role of language has always occupied a place of special significance (Ch. 4), and the work of Piaget is generally accorded particular importance (Ch. 5). Witkin's theory has commanded unusual attention in cross-cultural research because of its attempt to bridge the areas of cognition and personality (Ch. 3). In the course of discussing these various topics, there will be several opportunities to look at the broader questions posed in this first chapter concerning political philosophy, social change and psychological theory. But the reader should be warned in advance that we will not be finding any very definite answers.

2
Values, motives and personality

The study of how man's behaviour is affected by his society and culture is the traditional province of anthropology. Partly because his is generally a one-man show investigating a community of which his colleagues have no prior knowledge, the anthropologist casts his net very wide. He looks at every facet of the society which appears distinctive: where they locate their dwellings and how they build them, what plants and animals they do and do not eat, how they manage and celebrate the crucial human episodes of birth, adolescence, marriage and death, their beliefs about disease and about supernatural forces, their social values and the sanctions they use to enforce them, their forms of artistic expression, and so on. In all this he 'look(s) for regularities among many aspects of human behaviour within a single society, and . . . expect(s) to find them because all these various acts are performed by human beings who in addition to their shared humanity share a common tradition, a common way of looking at the world' (Mead, 1949:45). There are two contrasting ways of explaining these regularities: with reference to *institutions* and with reference to *modal personality types*.

The institutional approach refers clearly to the behaviour of groups and lies at the centre of sociology (see B5). An institution may be defined as 'the organized system of practices and social roles developed about a value or series of values, and the machinery evolved to regulate the practices and administer the rules' (Reuter, 1941:113). It is easy enough to recognize how this characterization applies to a modern political or economic institution such as a parliament or a bank, but the same analysis is used by social scientists to explain regularities in less obviously formalized systems of behaviour. Thus the family and football can also be described as institutions, the one concerned, among other things, with sexual intercourse and the upbringing of children, the other with recreation and entertainment. The description of just what practices and roles are laid down as desirable (or prescribed) by the institutions of a society in various fields of life provides one sort of explanatory framework for understanding why people in that society behave in the way they do.

Personality, on the other hand, is an individual characteristic and has been the subject of a wide variety of approaches since Freud's classic psychoanalytic theory was developed at the beginning of this century (see D1, D3 and C3). I shall follow the conventional definition here, formulated by Child (1968) as: 'the internally determined consistencies underlying a person's behaviour . . . the enduring differences among people in so far as they are attributable to stable internal characteristics rather than to differences in their life situation' (82). This concept is thus designed principally to account for individual differences. If we are to use it in explaining why people in one cultural group behave differently from those in another group, it is necessary to suppose that a certain type of individual predominates in one group whereas another type predominates in the other. Generally this predominance is conceived as a matter of numbers, and the statistical expression 'modal' (derived from the French word for fashion) is used to indicate that a culture's modal personality is the commonest type it produces. According to this approach, it is the inherent dispositions of this modal type of person which account for regularities in the group's behaviour patterns.

Theories of modal personality bear certain disturbing similarities to popular stereotypes. They focus attention on what is common to all the members of a group, playing down variations within the group and emphasizing differences between one group and another. Moreoever the delineation of modal personality is generally a highly intuitive matter. It 'is not a composite derived statistically from distributions of individual scores . . . but rather, a hypothetical reconstruction of a common structure posited interpretively from a series of individual patterns' (Inkeles and Levinson, 1969: 455). Many culture-and-personality theorists are conscious of the problem. Thus Levine (1973: 10) writes:

Group stereotypes are 'psychological' in the sense that they reduce complex national societies to an image of an individual – the Englishman, the Mexican, the Arab – and attribute to such images qualities such as might characterize a person – unfriendly, lazy, cunning, belligerent, sensuous ... Such characterizations have often been dangerous and irresponsible oversimplifications of complex realities. War, for instance, cannot be properly understood in terms of 'warlike' and 'peace-loving' peoples but only by taking into account the economic, social political, and psychological processes that produce it.

How then do such theorists escape the compelling analogy between popular stereotypes and their view that enduring personality dispositions lie at the root of cross-cultural differences in behaviour? We can identify three major lines of argument on this point. The first is simply that popular stereotypes are prejudiced, i.e. based on inadequate information, whereas the anthropologist has made a careful study of the group he is attempting to describe. This is a rather weak argument since it requires us to accept on faith the ability of the academic observer to adopt a more objective stance. The second argument is that the modal personality is not so extreme as the stereotype. The dispositions it describes are relative, not absolute, in their likelihood of producing a certain category of behaviour, in the extent to which they endure in the face of various social pressures and in the frequency with which they occur in different populations. The third argument goes a step further by allowing that a cultural group may produce more than one typical personality. This 'multi-modal' conception, however, threatens to undermine the whole approach. For we may then enquire which social forces within the culture are responsible for each particular type. And if these forces can be identified

it may well be that intranational groupings such as intellectuals or workers, have more in common psychologically with groupings of the same status in other nations [and cultures] than they have with their compatriots of higher [or lower] status. (Inkeles and Levinson, 1969:457)

Much of psychological theory about personality has been concerned with how various dispositions are interrelated or organized within the individual person (the so-called dynamics of personality). In a complementary way anthropological theory has focused on the integration of institutions within a society. The analogy between these two systems plays an important part in early writing about culture and personality. Thus Benedict (1934:46) writes that 'a culture, like an individual, is a more or less consistent pattern of thought and action. Within each culture there come into being characteristic purposes not necessarily shared by other types of society'. And she talks of a society as having 'emotional and intellectual mainsprings' and 'unconscious canons of choice'.

In her analysis of American Indian cultures, for instance, Benedict postulates, following Nietzsche's discussion of ancient Greek tragedy, two diametrically opposed sets of values: the Dionysian 'desire to achieve excess' and the Apollonian preference for 'the middle of the road'. The value-systems centred around these contrasting poles are sometimes presented as characterizing *practices*, i.e. recurrent patterns of behaviour, sometimes as features of individuals, sometimes as features of institutions. She describes the customs of the Pueblos as Apollonian: they make, for instance, as little as possible of the death of a spouse in order to minimize the pain of bereavement. By contrast, Plains Indians' customs on such occasions include Dionysian outbursts of grief, even extending to self-injury and other displays of aggression.

What is the relation between the individual's motives and the society's traditions in this respect? Benedict writes:

> These two attitudes at death are familiar types of contrasted behaviour, and most individuals recognize the congeniality of one or the other. The Pueblos have institutionalized the one, and the Plains the other . . . in one culture he [the individual] finds the one emotion already channeled for him, and in the other the other. Most human beings take the channel that is ready made in their culture. (1934:113)

But why does this happen? Is it because the custom expresses the commonest personality disposition of the people in that society, or is it that we can best express ourselves by adopting one of the institutionalized roles which our society acknowledges? The second alternative has been developed in great detail by Goffman (see F3). Society, in his view, understands the individual 'as a multiple-role-performer rather than as a person with a particular role', and hence 'as a person of many identifications' (1961:142). The image of himself that an individual presents is largely constrained by his immediate social situation. 'During interaction the individual is expected to possess certain attributes, capacities, and information which,

23

taken together, fit together into a self that is at once coherently unified and appropriate for the occasion' (Goffman, 1967:105). The extent to which individuals conform with these moral expectations of the culture will determine the nature of social encounters. But the expectations themselves depend not so much on individual dispositions as on the principles of a given social organization.

Levine (1973), on the other hand, argues for a distinction between behaviour which conforms with cultural expectations, and the inner experience which disposes the individual to behave in certain ways. He analyses in some detail the account by an American anthropologist (whose home culture recognizes bereavement in the Apollonian mode) of her reactions when faced with social behaviour in a Philippines community where the Dionysian mode prevails:

> In making a condolence call according to instructions, she suffers an 'almost paralysing embarrassment' that she relates to having been raised as an American. In other words, her emotional reactions – which are psychophysiological processes – have been so thoroughly programmed by her earlier normative environment that when she attempts to behave according to a different set of norms, even while knowing that what she is doing is appropriate and that an anthropologist is supposed to conform to local custom, she experiences internal resistance and discomfort. . . . [Thus an] outsider . . . can usually learn to behave in accordance with the host group's explicit customary rules and even empathize with their hopes and fears, but without acquiring the spontaneous feelings and beliefs that give these rules and motives deeper meanings and a culturally distinctive style of organization and integration. (1973:18–19)

Let us accept, for the sake of argument, that the individual's internal disposition can be studied independently of the social situations in which it is expressed. How might the cultural environment come to influence such personality dispositions? Clearly there are many avenues for such an influence. Each social encounter is rich in cues to behave in the culturally prescribed way. Every time the individual conforms he will receive confirmation of the appropriateness of his behaviour (or, as Behaviourists would term it, social reinforcement, see B1). Models of the prescribed behaviour will occur frequently in his experience for him to imitate. And more or less explicit instructions in how to behave on such occasions are directed at him through folk-tales, dances, pictures and religious activities. The 'consistent pattern' of the culture converges at every point to instil the right disposition.

Nevertheless, most theory on this subject has laid special emphasis on the environment in the early years of life. This bias arises undoubtedly from the tradition started by Freud, who assigned the essential processes of character formation to the oral, anal and phallic stages before the age of five (see C3, D3, F3). By confining their attention to this period, theorists are naturally led to emphasize some cultural institutions more than others. Religious ideology, for instance, is likely to have much less direct impact on very young children than the structure of the family. Thus a topic of central importance in this field has been the process of *socialization*, by which child-rearing practices are conceived as shaping the kind of personality which in adulthood will be harmonious with the norms of the society.

The best-known study in this field is that of Whiting and Child (1953), whose theoretical framework has since formed the basis of an ambitious study of child-rearing practices across six widely separate cultural groups: a Gusii farming community in Kenya, a Rajput neighbourhood in northern India, a coastal village in Okinawa (near Japan), a Mixtec Indian barrio in Mexico, an Ilocos barrio in the Philippines, and a small-town New England community in the USA (Whiting, 1963). The original study, unlike its sequel, was conducted 'at a distance' by culling material from the Human Relations Area Files at Harvard University and other published reports by anthropologists on small-scale rural communities. Two kinds of information were extracted from these records concerning 75 different societies: child-rearing practices and customs relating to illness. The latter were considered to be 'for the most part magical and unrealistic' and thus 'will tend to be those that are best learned or most often created because they resemble the fantasies to which the members of a society would individually be led by the personality characteristics they have in common' (Whiting and Child, 1953:120–1).

The sequence of cause and effect which this research postulates is illustrated in Fig. 2.1. The factors linked by solid arrows are those listed by Whiting (1963). But the original study sought to measure only the statistical correlation (see p. 121) between certain child-rearing practices and theories of disease. The fact that they found a number of significant correlations is, by their own admission, difficult to interpret with any certainty, since (a) where a relationship was demonstrated, an opposite sequence of cause and effect (with the cultural product determining the child-rearing practice) is often just as plausible an explanation as the one which they propose; (b) it is unclear whether the failures to find correlations in some cases are due to inadequate measures or to inadequate theory. It is for these reasons that they and their colleagues initiated the wider programme of new field research in which child and adult behaviour would be directly observed to give a clearer measure of the central concept of personality. But even with

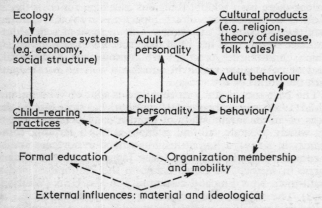

Fig. 2.1 *Culture, behaviour and personality interactions*

better measures this kind of research is problematic. Almost everywhere in the world today, societies are no longer self-contained, so that we need to add to the matrix a number of external influences; notably we have to consider those arising from the introduction of modern technology which creates a demand for schools, labour migration and all that follows. Some of these are shown at the bottom of Fig. 2.1 following Frijda and Jahoda, who contend 'that an intricate system of interlocking variables such as presented in [this] figure . . . defies causal analysis by the methods presently at our disposal; it also invalidates the assumption of linear causal sequences' (1966:114).

One conclusion we may draw from the numerous uncertainties in this field is that the attempt to relate a whole culture to personality patterns is over-ambitious. Fig. 2.1 suggests the outline of a grand design to which research might build up gradually. But each arrow in the figure requires careful study on its own. We need, for instance, to know not only which aspects of culture impinge on the child's development but also exactly how each exercises its influence. Arising from Freud's account of oral fixation in character development, great interest has surrounded cross-cultural variations in weaning. But the theoretical significance of this environmental change has not been agreed in detail. The age at which it occurs and the severity with which it is enforced are generally considered to be crucial factors. But clearly not only do these interact with each other in complex ways, but other factors such as the presence of a nurturant grandmother or elder sister must also greatly affect the psychological impact of weaning on the child. Bottle-feeding introduces still further complications by separating the pleasure of sucking from that of contact with the mother.

If the influence of cultural practice needs further elaboration, the measurement of personality presents even more difficult problems. Even within Western populations the development of personality tests has been a controversial topic (see D3). As one recent review remarks:

> In no other area of testing has there been such an overwhelming flood of articles, books, dissertations, research monographs, and tests. . . . In no case, however, has the accumulated research produced an enduring body of generally accepted knowledge concerning the validities of the test under study. We are still at the stage where every test, regardless of its merits and deficiencies, is considered useful by some and useless by others. (Buros, 1970:20–26)

Indeed there is little agreement about what sort of criteria should be applied in judging the validity of a personality test (Vernon, 1964).

While part of the controversy can be traced to basic theoretical and practical differences among researchers' orientations, the failure of most studies to yield convincing results may well be due in part to a rather simple conceptual flaw in the notion of a personality test. Although its objective is to gauge enduring dispositions, the test itself collects information over a very limited timespan and in a limited situation. Thus the dispositions expressed by an individual, whether openly or implicitly, in the context of a one-hour interview, with an unfamiliar doctor, in a clinic or a classroom, form the basis of the test's assessment of how that individual is likely to behave in a whole variety of different situations in which he has not been observed, and on future occasions when his mood may be greatly altered.

The significance of this limitation in 'predictive power' of a single test is especially marked in cross-cultural work. Not only does the test situation now differ in uncharted respects from the individual's range of life situations, but that real-world range is liable to differ in systematic ways across the cultural groups being compared. Moreover cultural differences will also partly determine the perceived structure of the testing situation because of 'the extreme variability in cultural norms regarding interpersonal privacy and self-revelation, conversing with foreigners or those of different status, responding verbally to novel problems posed by others' (Levine, 1973:77) etc.

Levine (1966), for instance, found a substantially higher incidence of achievement imagery in the dreams reported to him by Nigerian secondary-school boys than Strangman (1967) obtained when the same procedure was administered to students of a suburban American high school.

> In retrospect it seems probable that the appearance of an American professor in the Nigerian schools inflated the frequency of achievement imagery for the whole sample, whereas the appearance of an American graduate student (who was a community resident) in the American school had no such effect. This is supported by the incidence of dreams of leaving Nigeria to study abroad. . . . (Levine, 1973:77–8)

Analogously, a history of different patterns of interaction with Europeans or teachers might have contributed to the finding that within Nigeria, Ibo students expressed greater achievement imagery than Hausa students.

The study of achievement motivation, the need to excel, is another major area of cross-cultural research (see D2). McClelland (1961), like Whiting and Child, set out to demonstrate a relationship between two aspects of a culture on the supposition that the link between them was a feature of modal personality. Interestingly enough the supposed causal influence on the degree of childrens' achievement orientation in this theory is the content of folk-tales, which in Whiting's model appears as an expression of adult personality (see Fig. 2.1). The fact that both these interpretations of folk-tales can be seen as plausible underlines the circularity of this kind of analysis: almost any global feature of a society is both an expressive product of the individuals in one generation and a constraining influence on later generations. McClelland, however, is careful to take account of the time factor in his theory. The fantasy expressed in children's story books published during the period 1920–29 is seen as a specific influence on the generation contributing to economic development between 1929 and 1950, whereas story books published from 1946 to 1955 should have no such impact on that generation. His estimate of economic development is the rate of increase in electrical output by a nation's total resources. Considering the deviousness of the argument, one cannot help being impressed by McClelland's (1961) results. Achievement imagery in the

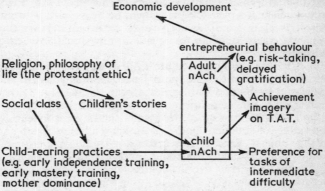

Fig. 2.2 *Some elements in McClelland's theory of achievement motivation and economic development*

1920s story books was correlated (see p. 121) across a sample of 23 non-tropical countries, $+\cdot53$ with increase in electrical output in the thirties and forties, whereas achievement imagery in the 1940s and 1950s books was negligibly correlated $(+\cdot03)$ with electrical output in the thirties and forties.

The detailed sequence of cause and effect in McClelland's theory is outlined in Fig. 2.2. Several steps in the argument can be questioned. Some political analysts, for example, would give less weight to the role of entrepreneurs in economic development. From a psychological perspective clearly what is lacking in the study cited above is any direct assessment of individual motivation. In the earlier work which identified the need for achievement (nAch) as a specific motive, the principal measuring device was the Thematic Apperception Test (TAT) (McClelland *et al.*, 1953). This is called a *projective test* because it consists of a series of deliberately vague pictures about which the testee is asked to tell stories, and the contents of the stories he tells are interpreted as a projection of the individual's most prevalent desires and fantasies (see D3 and F3). Several studies have shown that if students are given instructions before this test which are calculated to arouse their concern with achievement, the stories they tell contain more frequent 'references to "standards of excellence" and to doing well, or wanting to do well, with respect to the standards' (McClelland, 1961:41). The fact that this sensitivity of the test to situational pressures has been observed for Brazilian as well as American students (Angelini, 1966) might seem to make it a plausible instrument for cross-cultural work. But it is clear from Levine's study of dream reports that it is extremely difficult to equate testing situations across cultures.

McClelland (1961) applied the TAT as well as various other tests to samples of schoolboys in Japan, Germany, Brazil and India and to samples of business executives in Italy, Turkey and Poland for comparison with American subjects. But although his discussion of the results shows great ingenuity, the variety of situations both in actual test administration and in the subjects' general lives makes any confident interpretation of them extremely hazardous. At one point we are warned that translation errors may have introduced 'non-comparability between countries' (1961:476) in rating the stories for achievement imagery. Elsewhere the suggestion is raised that 'the German school atmosphere . . . might have been more achievement oriented and well-disciplined than . . . American college groups' (1961:477). On the other hand we are asked to consider two alternative explanations of why Turkish businessmen, unlike those in other countries, did not score higher in nAch than their compatriots entering professional careers. It might be because the professional sample included a high proportion of men who had left home at an early age and may therefore have been 'atypically high in nAch for Turkey' (1961:263). Or it might be because 'the lower ranks of business management in Turkey . . . are not attracting efficiently the men with high nAch' (1961:264).

Maehr (1974) has pointed out that the actual behaviour indicative of a motive to achieve success is controlled to a very marked degree by the situation in which the behaviour occurs. The best situation for eliciting achievement-oriented behaviour (or even fantasy) may vary quite considerably from one cultural group to another. 'Black' American ghetto culture, for instance, probably favours competition on the basket-ball court much more than in the classroom, while Navajo cultural norms may prohibit achievement orientation when face to face competition is implied. If an individual is to express a desire to succeed he must appraise the task situation (whether real or imaginary) as relevant to his own aspirations and within the scope of his possible control. Likewise in the study of risk-taking, birth control may seem a cautious policy by the standards of British culture, but for Ugandan students it may constitute a risky violation of conventional norms (Wober and Bukombi, 1973). This is more than a problem of measurement: it also relates to how we interpret cross-cultural differences in economic activity. Before jumping to the conclusion that economic stagnation arises from a lack of individuals driven by an inherent disposition to succeed, we need to understand the incentives and constraints which are effective in different communities. For 'while the activities of man constitute the essence of economic growth, the social system structures both the opportunities and contingencies of those activities' (Kunkel, 1970:101) (see B5).

The study of nAch reflects a widely held concern in cross-cultural studies of motivation with the adaptability of people in developing countries to the demands of large-scale modern economies. Many sociological observers have expressed the view that urbanization and industrialization not only alter the structure of society, but also involve changes in moral values and social motives. A pervasive difficulty in the study of these changes (which we will also find in Chapters 4 and 5 in the study of intellectual processes connected with Western culture) arises from the very widespread 'assumption that modernity is not only distinctive from but superior to whatever preceded it' (Berger, Berger and Kellner, 1973: 11). Yet the technology and bureaucracy which have shaped so many of the distinctive qualities of modern life evolved almost exclusively in the context of Western civilization. Thus Inkeles (1966) lists nine characteristics of 'modern man' which on his own admission have much in common with the values expressed in the literature of Ancient Greece and Elizabethan England. Yet he concludes that 'whether we view them as positive or negative we must recognize that these are qualities that are fostered by modern institutions, qualities that in many ways are required of the citizens of modern societies' (1966:150). A contrasting viewpoint is adopted by Berger and his colleagues, who argue that institutional processes and clusters of consci-

31

ousness are often presented as a 'package', although some elements are necessary while others are historical accidents. A major focus of their analysis is on 'which packages of modernity can be "taken apart" and which cannot be' (Berger *et al.*, 1973: 22).

One of the most attractive lines of enquiry into this difficult topic is to investigate the values held by people who have entered occupations within the matrix of 'modern' institutions but whose early socialization was in the context of a non-industrialized rural society. The most readily accessible populations of this kind are students in institutions of higher learning outside the Western world. Rather than trying to uncover their 'unconscious motives' or their 'deeper personality', studies in this vein have concentrated on conscious, and perhaps more superficial, attitudes. The results of such surveys are often intuitively plausible. Thus Sumotirto (1962) found that Indonesian high-school students attached greater importance to social responsibility than to individualism by contrast with Western students; and urban and 'upper class' students within his samples were more likely to recognize individualism as a realistic (rather than ideal) value than rural students. Similarly Feather and Hutton (1974) found that Papua New Guinea students ranked social recognition as a more important value than self-respect and placed obedience above independence, while Australian students ordered both these pairs of values in the opposite direction.

It is difficult in these studies to distinguish between the direct effects of socialization and a self-consciously adopted stance consonant with national or sub-cultural ideology as it is expressed in the public media. The volatility of electoral attitudes revealed by public opinion polls should warn us against reading too deep a significance into the 'values' revealed by such surveys. Another danger is illustrated by Feather and Hutton's study, which required students to place in rank order two sets of 18 values. They interpret the priority given by Papua New Guinea students to national security, salvation and obedience as 'a reflection of strongly felt safety and security needs' in 'a less affluent, developing country'; whereas the values preferred by Australian students (including self-respect, sense of accomplishment, mature love and being broad-minded and independent) are seen as 'more closely related to needs concerning love, competence and self-actualization which, according to Maslow (1954) (see D3), would be more likely to become prepotent once the more basic

32

physiologic and safety and security needs have been satisfied' (Feather and Hutton, 1974:100). But it is doubtful whether the particular 'higher needs' which feature in the lists are as representative of those which command concern in Papua New Guinea as they are for the Western culture of Australia. The authors note, for instance, that a local resident 'asked why values concerning generosity, loyalty, and justice were not on the lists' (p. 102). These are hardly safety and security values in Maslow's usage, and if they were ranked higher by Papua New Guinea students than by Australians, they would belie these authors' attempt to stratify the two cultures in terms of the level of needs they emphasize.

Superficial and restricted though attitude surveys tend to be, they may throw some light on the question of how far the modern 'package' can be taken apart. A common assumption is that when different cultures meet, 'incompatibility will arise between what exists and what is new', not only because of the different assumptions of mythology and science but also because new ideas 'change the effects of social rules and thus upset the structure of society' (Kavadias, 1966:365–70). We should not overlook, however, that in technologically advanced nations, scientific concepts still coexist in most of the population with mythological religious beliefs. Jahoda (1970) reports in a study of Ghanaian students between 1955 and 1968 'a partial return to traditional West African cosmological notions', including the existence of witchcraft as a power and fear of magical threats against oneself, and concludes that 'the younger generation of Ghanaian students have achieved . . . a state of "cognitive coexistence" between modern ideas and values and some traditional African beliefs' (1970:128–9). A similar compromise has often been described in the institutional religious practices of communities where one of the proselytizing religions, Christianity or Islam, has superseded an earlier, animist cult as the officially recognized doctrine. Some familiar examples are the Christmas tree and the throwing of confetti at Christian weddings.

While this conclusion may give us hope for the possibility of compromise in cross-cultural and international relations, other reports present a gloomier account of the psychological consequences of culture contact. Kavadias (1966:368) for instance contends that in developing countries the 'message of modernization' is seldom fully understood and generally fails to be properly assimilated within the pre-existing culture. This leads to:

phenomena of frustration and anxiety: the peoples concerned are torn by conflicting emotions aroused by their awareness of the fact that they ought to adopt the innovation but cannot adapt it to their situation. . . .

If this kind of reaction is a direct product of the impact of Western culture, we should expect to find in the cities of these countries both exceptionally high rates of mental illness and also mental illness of a distinctive kind (see F3). Evidence on the latter point is easier to evaluate than that on the question of frequency.

Leighton and his associates (1963) found that Yoruba people in a Nigerian city presented symptoms of mental disorder more frequently than Yoruba living in rural villages, and attribute their findings to the disintegration of traditional society and culture in the urban situation. Many changes occur, however, when a person migrates from the country to the town. Western-type medical services are more available, and the institutions of employment may be more permissive of 'time off' for any kind of illness than the social context of a rural community. Although there may be real (even physical) causes of mental illness, the frequency and form in which it appears are probably largely controlled by the range of acceptable roles which are sanctioned by the society. There seems to be no way of determining, when two groups show different frequencies of a mentally abnormal behaviour pattern, whether the conditions in one group tend to cause the disorder or merely to permit its expression in that form.

Most cross-cultural studies of the incidence of psychiatric disorders are based on records of patients who have found their way into mental hospitals or out-patient clinics. To interpret these studies we need to bear in mind both the scarcity of such facilities in most economically under-developed countries and also the various alternatives which each society provides for the relief of mental suffering. In Europe many emotional crises are referred to priests; in Africa the traditional healer plays a similar role. In some cases the community may not consider deviant certain symptoms which the Western clinician takes as indications of mental illness. Thus German (1972) reports that in African mental hospitals until recently few cases of psychotic depression (see F3) were seen, possibly because they tended to be kept at home; and relatively few cases of epilepsy were seen because in many African societies this is classified as an African illness not understood by European medicine (Orley, 1970). On the other hand a rather high proportion of acute transient psychoses are treated, in which the patients (principally men) experience vivid hallucinations and are often aggressive. Such cases might often qualify for a diagnosis of schizophrenia in Western patients, were it not for their extremely good prospects of recovery.

Since statistics on the disorders which are not referred to hospitals are very scarce, we must be cautious in interpreting the different patterns of frequency found in different societies. This applies also to objectively identifiable behaviours such as suicide, which may be regularly concealed from the authorities by a community which abhors the act in countries with very limited law-enforcement agencies. Nevertheless plausible accounts can be offered of how cultural values enter into the particular form mental disorders take. German, for instance, comments on the rarity of self-directed symptoms of guilt and worthlessness in African patients as follows:

> It may be that ideas of personal responsibility and hence ideas of personal guilt can only appear when the group as a locus of identification is given up in favour of an individual identity associated with a competitive and aggressive attitude to other people. (1972:472)

It should be emphasized, however, that while studies of cultural values may throw light on psychiatric practice, clinical findings can be of little assistance in understanding the overall impact of culture on behaviour. This is because we do not have at present an adequate theory of how abnormal behaviour is related to the behaviour of the general population (see F3).

I have not begun in this short chapter to do justice to the variety of theoretical interpretations relating culture to personality (see C3). Instead I have dwelt on some of the conceptual problems which dominate this field. There can be little doubt that motives and attitudes are closely related to cultural norms, but the task of analysing that relationship into a sequence of causes and effects has so far proved to be remarkably difficult.

3
Field-dependency across cultures: cognitive style or perceptual skill?

Psychological theories are often concerned with processes and structures which cannot be directly observed. The more abstract or general the psychological characteristic we are studying, the more indirect are the measurements we make of it.

Consider the specific response of drawing a margin with pencil and ruler along the left-hand side of a page of lined paper. If we observe that two children in their first year at school differ substantially, over a series of such responses, in the degree to which they orient their margins parallel to the edge of the page, we might be tempted to attribute this difference to an underlying psychological characteristic called perceptual-motor coordination. If, on the other hand, we observe a similar difference between two students in their first year at college, we will probably be more inclined to attribute the difference to an alternative underlying characteristic called carelessness. In both cases we could describe the response as a *measure* (or indicator) of a psychological characteristic, in one case an ability, in the other case an attitude or disposition of personality. If we included the margin-ruling response as an item in a test, we could score it in terms of the number of degrees of displacement from true parallel: the greater the average displacement of an individual's response, the less efficient her perceptual-motor coordination, or – in the case of the college students – the greater her carelessness.

The phenomenon of a variation in behaviour like this which can reasonably be attributed to either cognitive or motivational factors is not at all unusual. It poses a very basic procedural problem in psychological research. If we wish to study a cognitive process, such as learning or perception, we must establish a level of motivation in our subjects which is sufficient to guarantee that they want to do their best in the test situation. If the subjects are rats, we may starve them for twenty-four hours and offer them food as a reward for choosing the correct turning in a maze; if they are college students we will normally be content with less drastic measures such as instructing them verbally: 'I want you to solve this problem as fast as you can'. Conversely, if we want to study a motivational process such as need for achievement (see Ch. 2) or anxiety, we need to be sure that the cognitive states necessary for understanding the task situation are present in all our subjects. A cat will not experience anxiety when a puff of air is delivered into its face from the food-bowl unless it has learned that the source of the air is normally a source of food, and unless it recognizes the source of the pleasant and unpleasant events as the same (Masserman, 1943). And we cannot claim to be measuring need for achievement in a child's response to the TAT (see Ch. 2) if she repeats the story of Little Red Riding Hood which she heard in school that morning, having failed to grasp that she is supposed to invent her own story for the picture.

These issues are of special concern in the present chapter because Witkin's (1959) concept of cognitive style is presented as a meeting point between cognition and motivation (see D3). Several lines of research have shown that people's motives affect their perception. For instance, social pressure, engineered by paying a group of collaborators to lie about what they see, results in an uninformed member of the group agreeing with their lies (Asch, 1955). Similar results have been reported with American, Brazilian, Lebanese, Hong Kong Chinese and Fijian college students, and somewhat higher levels of conformity in Rhodesian African and Fijian Indian students (Whittaker and Meade, 1967; Chandra, 1973). Close questioning of the students who took part in the American experiments suggested that the desire to conform did not just lead them to lie about what they saw: it actually caused them to see what the others said they saw. Some motives are carried over into the laboratory from experience in the real world. Children of poor families tend to overestimate the physical size of coins more than children of richer families (Tajfel, 1957; Munroe et al., 1969). Witkin's theory is that the personality of the individual structures her perception in a similar way. How she perceives the physical world is related to the style of interaction she has developed with the social world.

Consider the tasks illustrated in Fig. 3.1. In order to solve these problems, the individual must impose a selected structure on a complex visual stimulus such as A or Y and analyse it into components (as shown in C) which break up the natural lines (or gestalt – see A4) of the whole figures. Witkin considers the ability to do this an indication of cognitive style. Those who fail he regards as people who tend to be passively dominated by their surroundings (field-dependent), those who succeed as more autonomous in their outlook on life (field-independent). We might suggest that in order to read this sort of personality dimension into the subjects' performance in such trivial activities, we must assume (as with the TAT) that the basic perceptual and intellectual skills required to comprehend the task are present throughout the population from which the subjects are drawn. Conversely if we were to consider the ability to solve these problems a purely cognitive skill, then we should have to assume that attitudes to the task, motivation to succeed etc, are fairly constant across the population. We will return to this dichotomy between personality disposition and cognitive skill when we examine the cross-cultural research using these tasks. Meanwhile we should note that many writers claiming to follow Witkin's theory seem to view the distinction as artificial.

Thus Okonji (1972) notes with approval that: 'Through the cognitive style approach to the study of psychological functioning one can glean the perceptual, intellectual and personality dimensions on the same mirror' (1972:2). In the normal course of development the individual is said increasingly to differentiate herself from the environment, and to analyse the environment into separate components within a coherent structure. Individual differences in this 'psychological differentiation' can be observed at any age level in the style of perceptual experience (global or analytic), in intellectual independence and flexibility, or in social conformity and personality dispositions. 'The field-dependent mode of perception is thus identified with earlier stages of growth and in this sense is more primitive' (Witkin, 1959). In spite of his generally negative portrayal of the field-dependent personality, however, Witkin (1959:54) has stressed that:

> it would be a mistake to infer that these traits [characteristic of field-independence] necessarily imply better adaptation to life situations, or absence of pathology . . . Perceptual style

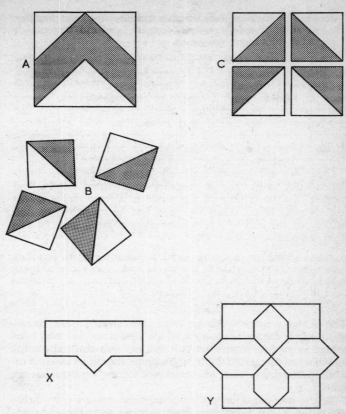

Fig. 3.1 *Koh's Block Design Copying Test and the Embedded Figures Test (EFT)*

In the block assembly version of Koh's design copying task, the first step is to turn all the blocks over until the appropriate sides are on top. With the blocks scattered as at B, the problem is then to rearrange them so as to copy the design A. C shows the four quadrants into which A must be analysed in order to solve the task.

Notice the similarity between this perceptual aspect of the task and the Embedded Figures Test (EFT). Here the task is to find shape X embedded in shape Y.

See text for a discussion of this similarity which may account for the finding by Witkin and others that children's scores on these two tests tend to be correlated.

does not by itself indicate whether a child will have a 'healthy' personality; it may, however, suggest the form that pathological developments may take.

This impartial stance, however, is thrown into question by the theory's treatment of child-rearing practices contributing to differences in cognitive style. The mothers of field-dependent boys are said to adopt a variety of strategies which hamper the growth of independence: they are over-protective and restrictive of exploration and originality; they administer discipline arbitrarily and impulsively, wavering between irrational threats and over-indulgence; and they lack confidence in themselves as mothers (Witkin, 1967).

Clearly a mother theoretically likely to promote field-dependency in her son is on every count listed here a 'bad mother' by the criteria of the modern Western mass media (e.g. Spock, 1970). Thus we need not be surprised to find Witkin, at the end of a review of cross-cultural work in this field, suggesting that:

> it is a challenge to future social action research to translate into forms appropriate to the school and other social settings, the processes which, in the child's early interpersonal relations in the family, have been found to foster development of an articulated cognitive style and self-differentiation. (1967:249)

The characteristics which we were told earlier do not 'necessarily imply better adaptation to life situations' are now presented as so important that cultural and sub-cultural groups which do not promote them in the home should be assisted by a supplementary diet of 'growth-fostering' techniques in school.

Before we consider the cross-cultural research on field-dependency, we must introduce another test: the rod-and-frame test (RFT). This, like the more elaborate body-adjustment test, is a special creation of Witkin's and concerns 'perception of the upright' (Witkin, 1959). The subject is seated in a completely dark room and presented with a luminous array like that shown in Fig. 3.2. The square frame and the rod within it can be rotated independently of each other. The subject instructs the experimenter to rotate the rod clockwise or anticlockwise until it appears to him to be exactly vertical, i.e. perpendicular with the floor which he cannot see. In some cases the subject's chair is also tilted to make it that much more difficult for him to judge where the true vertical lies. Some individuals tend to align the rod at right angles to the frame

(Fig. 3.2a). Witkin considers that their response, dominated by the gestalt of the visual field – i.e. the frame – is an indication of field-dependency. Other individuals ignore the frame and adjust the rod close to the true vertical (Fig. 3.2b). The closer a subject's average adjustment over a series of trials to true vertical, the more field-independent that subject is considered to be.

The main evidence that this RFT is measuring the same psychological characteristic as the EFT shown in Fig. 3.1 is statistical. Those subjects who gained field-independent scores

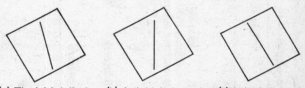

(a) The initial display (b) A field-independent (c) A field-dependent
                             response   response

Fig. 3.2 *Witkin's Rod and Frame Test (RFT)*

The rod rotates about an axis central to the square frame. Both rod and frame are luminous in an otherwise totally dark room.

on one test tended in the early research to gain similar scores on the other. Table 3.1 shows the correlation coefficients (see p. 121) obtained for various samples between scores on the two tests. Note that the correlations are higher for male samples than for females and that for African samples most of the correlations are low and statistically insignificant. One major finding in the Western research which has received a lot of attention in cross-cultural theorizing was the tendency for females to gain on average more field-dependent scores than males. Although Witkin has pointed out the possibility that this sex difference might have a genetic basis, most of the literature has related this finding to the patterns of child-rearing cited above. In Western cultures there is probably a tendency for mothers to adopt a more protective approach towards their daughters than their sons, and to encourage less aggression or self-assertion in girls.

The child-rearing determinants of cognitive style form the basis for one interpretation of cross-cultural differences in performance on the tests of field-dependency. Since this

Table 3.1 Correlations between RFT and EFT scores by various populations

USA children				African children

USA children

Age	mixed sex	male	female
10	0·31*	0·60**	0·55**
11		0·36	0·60**
12	0·51**	0·56**	0·49**
13	0·55**	0·48**	0·64**
15	0·31*	0·56**	—0·15
17	0·42**	0·52**	0·40*

(Witkin et al., 1962) (Witkin et al., 1967)

USA adults

	male	female
(Witkin et al., 1962)	0·64**	0·21
	0·63**	0·30*
	0·42*	0·37*
(Witkin et al., 1967) (College students)	0·76**	0·26*

African children

mixed sex, age 12–17		
Zambia (urban)	0·29*	(Siann, 1972)
male, age 4–6		
Uganda (urban)	non-significant	(Okonji, 1972)

African children & adults

mixed sex 12-year-olds and adults		
Nigeria (rural)	—0·21	(Okonji, 1969)

African adults

male		
Nigeria (industrial employees)	0·18	(Wober, 1966)
	0·21	(Wober, 1967)
mixed sex		
Nigeria (University students)	0·47**	(Okonji, 1969)

Asterisks indicate levels of statistical significance: *0·05; **0·01
See Appendix for a brief explanation of the correlation coefficient.

approach has not modified the original theory in any significant way, I shall call it the *Witkin theory*. Berry (1966) has compared the performance of two totally separated cultural groups in different parts of the world (North American Eskimo and West African Temne); Dawson (1967) has compared two cultural groups within the same country (Temne and Mende in Sierra Leone); and Okonji (1969) has compared two groups from the same West African tribe at different levels of urbanization. In each case the results have been interpreted in terms of the child-rearing methods practised by the two groups under consideration. Following Witkin's suggestions, these authors hypothesized that cultures which encourage parents to instil conformity and social dependency in their children will produce individuals who are by and large more field-dependent in cognitive style than cultures where the norms encourage early autonomy and exploration in children. Performance on the tests is seen as reflecting a deeply-rooted feature of the individual's personality.

In sharp contrast to the Witkin theory stands the *perceptual skill* approach. The RFT and EFT and Koh's Blocks Test are based on the Gestalt laws of perception (Gottschaldt, 1926; Goldstein and Scheerer, 1941; see A4). Their difficulty arises from the need to suppress the powerful impression of the overall figure and concentrate on one or more components of the figure in isolation from the rest. The ability to perform such a task will be enhanced by familiarity with the ways in which geometrical shapes combine to form larger configurations. School geometry, for instance, teaches that the area of a right-angled triangle is half the product of two of its sides by helping children to *see* that the same triangle, rotated, can be laid against the hypotenuse of this one to make a rectangle. In the same way the schoolchild learns that a square can be broken up in her visual imagination into four equal triangles with their apices meeting at the intersection of the diagonals (see Fig. 3.3). The perceptual skill theory focuses attention on these specific abilities and hypothesizes that an environment which provides many opportunities to acquire them will produce individuals generally better able to solve the RFT, EFT and Koh's Blocks Test. This approach has been elaborated by Sherman (1967) for sex differences and by Siann (1972) for cross-cultural differences.

An intermediate position between these two theoretical approaches was developed by Wober (1966, 1967). He noted that a cornerstone of the Witkin theory is the close correlation across individuals between scores on EFT and scores on RFT. Since both are very indirect measures of the theoretical concept of cognitive style, they must be seen to correlate quite highly if we are to suppose that they measure a single dimension called field-dependency. Wober (1967) found that for two samples of Nigerian male apprentices the correlation between the two tests was low and non-significant (see *Table 3.1*). He argued from this that they were measuring different

Fig. 3.3 *Embedded figures in school geometry*

Children learn in school geometry that triangles A and B are the same shape rotated and embedded within the rectangle; likewise triangles P, Q, R and S within the square.

characteristics. RFT, he suggested, might still be measuring field-dependency in the West African population, but EFT was probably measuring mainly the degree of skill acquired in the visual medium through Western-style education. He noted, in support of this, that EFT scores (unlike RFT scores) were significantly correlated with the number of years of formal education his subjects had undergone.

The way in which RFT measures cognitive style in West Africa is different according to Wober (1966) from the way in which it measures it in Western cultures. Cognitive style, he suggests, is elaborated in the sensory medium emphasized by the prevailing culture. In the West the 'Gutenberg Galaxy' (McLuhan, 1962) unleashed by the printed word has raised the visual modality's significance out of all proportion in relation to the other senses. But in West African culture it is music, dance and the plastic arts which predominate, so that the sensory modalities of hearing, proprioception (the sense of our own movements) and touch receive greatest emphasis as media for the development of cognitive skills such as field-independence. Thus in the RFT, Western subjects (who represent a visual 'sensotype') deal with the problem in visual terms, while West African subjects (with their somatic 'sensotype') deal with it in proprioceptive terms.

Before considering the evidence relating to these different interpretations, we should note the broad differences in their views of how culture affects human behaviour. The Witkin theory resembles those of Whiting and McClelland discussed in Chapter 2 in postulating an influence of culture on the individual's personality. Field-dependency is presented as a pervasive characteristic of the individual derived from her interaction with other human beings and affecting her manner of perception in all the fields of life. Wober's theory of senso-types sees each culture as providing a certain realm within which the personality can develop in various ways. Individual differences in field-dependency, for instance, may be found in West Africa just as in the USA, but the sensory media in which cognitive differentiation takes place are different for the two cultures. The perceptual skill theory resembles the Witkin theory in assigning culture a more active, formative role than Wober does, but it suggests that the focus of a culture's influence is more limited to particular activities. The upbringing of a forest hunter will promote skills of discrimination (in vision, hearing and smell) which are quite different from those instilled in a Western classroom. For instance, the ability to separate an item from its perceptual context in EFT or RFT may be, in some abstract sense, conceptually equivalent to the ability which the hunter has acquired to spot an animal camouflaged in a thicket, but the perceptual skills involved are not the same. Hence Western architects will need protection in the African forest and African hunters will need assistance at the Western drawing-board.

Dawson (1967) draws together the perceptual skill and Witkin theories in the following manner:

> It was considered that educational achievement, intelligence, experience of a carpentered environment [see ch. 6] . . . would be relevant variables in the acquisition of cues to perceive pictorial material in 3-D [see Ch. 6] up to a certain level, beyond which field dependence was expected to be the major limiting variable. (1967:118)

An alternative view might reverse the order of priorities: individual differences in personality can account for a certain range of variations in performance on tasks like the EFT and RFT, but beyond this a major limiting variable will be the degree to which an individual is equipped with the necessary perceptual and cognitive skills required to understand the task. Siann (1972:92), for instance, presents evidence that one category of the schoolchildren she tested were

disoriented and their responses are seen as randomly distributed and the following anecdotal evidence appears to support this: after the RFT trials a large number of subjects in this group asked the Zambian experimenter in the vernacular why the other experimenter [a European] was trying to 'confuse' them.

One difficulty in separating the two extreme hypotheses arises from the fact that those cultural groups which favour the socialization techniques theoretically calculated to promote field-independence are generally also more similar to the West in the perceptual skills which their physical habitat and artistic traditions promote. Thus Berry (1971:328) concludes from ethnographic studies that:

> hunting peoples are expected to possess good visual discrimination and spatial skill, and their cultures are expected to be supportive of the development of these skills through the presence of a high number of 'geometrical spatial' concepts, [encoded in the language – see Ch. 4] a highly developed and generally shared arts and crafts production, and socialization practices whose content emphasizes independence and self reliance, and whose techniques are supportive and encouraging of separate development.

Thus, whether we emphasize perceptual learning or early independence training we are led to predict that the Eskimo people of Baffin Island will score higher on EFT and Koh's Blocks than the Temne people of Sierra Leone. And this is just what Berry (1966) found. Likewise when Dawson tells us that 'Temne tribal values are much more aggressive than the western type values of the Mende' (1967:122), we may legitimately wonder whether the latter group's superior performance on EFT may not arise from greater exposure to Western artefacts rather than, as Dawson suggests, from less severe maternal control.

Okonji (1969) makes the same point in relation to the performance on EFT and RFT of undergraduates at the University of Nigeria whose childhood was spent in urban areas, which was superior to that of their fellow-students raised in rural areas. On the one hand:

> it is argued . . . that besides the well-known fact that in most cases there is greater stress on conformity to social norms in rural areas than in urban areas, there are reasons connected with socialization ideologies and practices [among the Ibo] which justify the view that urban-bred children will tend to develop more field-independent characteristics than children bred in rural areas. (1969:296)

But, on the other hand, the question may be raised:

is it the mere fact of living in an urban area at all, no matter the age at which residence begins, or the total length of residence, or attending better schools or being brought up by literate parents in a particular manner or all of these that makes the urban subjects in the sample more field-independent? (1969:304)

This problem is a very common one in all scientific research: we are faced with (at least) two 'confounded variables' (see A8): child-rearing practices and formal education. We would like to know how much each factor affects performance on these tasks, but in the normal course of events both factors vary together. Several studies have tried to separate them by careful sampling. Thus both Berry (1966) and Dawson (1967) included in their samples groups of people from the same cultural background with different levels of formal, Western-type education, and found that Western-educated subjects reliably scored higher on the various tests, including EFT and Koh's Blocks, than those who had not been to school. They argue, however, that education is only part of the story: over and above which cultural differences in socialization are important determinants of cognitive style. But we know that the quality of school education varies dramatically from one school to another and we cannot discount the possibility that the cross-cultural differences which remain after 'controlling for level of education' (as, for instance, Okonji, 1969 did by comparing two groups of university students) are still the result of differences in the specific education received.

A more precise approach was adopted by Okonji (1972) in a study comparing two groups of four-to-six-year-old urban Ugandan boys. Their socio-economic background was very different, one group coming from families with highly educated, professional parents most of whom provided Western-type toys for their children and employed ayahs to care for them when the parents went to work, the other group from families where the parents had little or no education, were less inclined to buy toys for the children and kept most of the child care to the mother. All forty-eight of the mothers were interviewed in depth about their child-rearing practices and later came to the laboratory where they were observed interacting with their sons in an experimental game. None of the behavioural categories recorded under direct observation differentiated between the two socio-economic status (s.e.s.) groups of mothers,

47

but three items on the interview questionnaire showed a reliable difference. The high s.e.s. mothers were more permissive of early signs of independence in their sons, more often stated that it was they rather than the father who took most decisions about the child, and rated their sons as more aggressive than the other group. The two groups of boys scored equally on Raven's Progressive Matrices (a spatial 'intelligence test'), but the high s.e.s. group scored significantly higher on the children's EFT and on RFT.

Now, by making such a fine-grain record of how the parents differed in child-rearing practice between the two groups, this study enables us to check on the relative validity of the two theories. If the social character of the mother–son relationship is critical we should find a close correlation between the scores on EFT and RFT and those variables which differentiate the two groups. The correlation coefficients, however, range from $-\cdot20$ to $+\cdot27$ and are all unreliable. Apparently none of the twenty-one indicators recorded about these mothers was appropriate to show a significant relation to performance on these tests. Unfortunately the results presented do not examine whether any physical variables, such as the presence of books and toys in the home, were related to test performance. But we may note in support of the perceptual skill theory that the RFT scores did not correlate reliably with either of the other tests, whereas scores on the two pictorial tests (Raven's Matrices and EFT) were significantly correlated ($r = +\cdot44$). Children who did well on one pictorial test tended to do well on the other, but performance on these tests was unrelated to performance on the RFT, which seems likely to demand quite different perceptual skills.

The greatest degree of control we can exercise over a variable is normally achieved by manipulating it ourselves. This approach was adopted by Siann (1972). She predicted that the skills acquired by boys in separating figures from a field would be confined to materials with which they were familiar and which they found interesting. So she devised two sets of embedded figures, one designed to be significant to boys, including pictures of a football match and a man in a sports car, and another significant to girls, including pictures of a woman sewing at a machine and a woman with a baby. In accordance with her prediction Zambian secondary school boys scored higher on the boy-significant test than girls, but failed to do so on the girl-significant test. She obtained the same pattern of results presenting overlapping outline drawings (see Ghent, 1956) of items with different sex-significance to young Zambian primary school children. These are quite striking results when viewed in the light of general difficulties experienced by Zambian children with pictorial materials (see Ch. 6). We must note, however, that the girls in Siann's samples did not score significantly higher than boys on the girl-significant tests, while boys continued to score higher than girls on the relatively neutral geometrical shape versions of these tests. The familiarity and 'significance' of the items thus may account for some of the sex differences in performance on these tests but it cannot account for all of them. It remains for this approach to be developed in relation to cross-cultural differences on EFT. Okonji (1971) and Serpell (1974) have shown that familiarity is relevant to such differences on other cognitive tasks (see Chs. 5 and 6).

The argument advanced by Wober (1967) is somewhat more complex than the other two theories we have been considering. With regard to the correlation between EFT scores and educational attainment his view is consonant with the perceptual skill theory. Western-type education clearly lays great emphasis on pictorial interpretation skills. But whether it develops the visual modality any more effectively *overall* than other cultures might be questioned. We will consider this issue in more detail in Chapter 6. Let us consider here his analysis of the RFT. In order to solve this problem, the subject has to relate his sense of the true upright (which in total darkness is derived from his body senses alone – see Gibson, 1966) to the orientation in space of a visual stimulus: the luminous rod. The central task, then, straddles two sensory realms, linking proprioceptive and visual information. Now when the frame is tilted out of alignment with the walls of the room, an additional source of visual information is provided, which is calculated to mislead. Likewise if the chair is tilted out of a normal orientation, misleading proprioceptive information is added. Wober suggests that the proprioceptive sensotype promoted by West African cultures equips the field-independent observer with the ability to resist the misleading cues from the tilted chair, whereas the Western, visual sensotype equips field-independent observers with the ability to resist the misleading visual cues from the tilted frame.

Based on these considerations Wober (1967) generated a strong theoretical prediction:

West African subjects would have better scores on tests where proprioceptivity was important [i.e. with tilted chair] (a)

49

relative to their scores on tests dependent on visuality [i.e. with tilted frame] and (b) relative to scores of Westerners on similar tests. (1967:31)

Confirmation of the first hypothesis is presented showing that, in his sample of eighty-six adult Nigerian manual workers, the average displacement of their responses from true vertical with body tilted and frame straight was about 1°, whereas with body straight and frame tilted it was about 11°. A smaller difference in the same direction is apparent in the response by American subjects, which he presents for comparison from Witkin and Asch (1948), with averages of about 4·6 degrees and 6 degrees respectively. 'Actually, the 4·6° figure is very much exaggerated by the results of four subjects who had extremely large errors. If these four cases are omitted, the mean error for the remaining 37 subjects drops to 2·7°' (Witkin and Asch, 1948:765). So far the only notable feature of the Nigerian results, then, is that the difference between the two conditions is somewhat more pronounced than that found with American subjects.

Wober's next step, however, is to compare the responses in each condition between the two samples. And here he finds support for hypothesis (b). Nigerians made less errors than Americans in the body-tilted-frame-erect condition. Now, in order to accept that these differences between the groups (which are statistically significant) reflect differences in the people tested, we need to be sure that the conditions under which they were tested were equivalent. This is very difficult to evaluate since the details of procedure are incomplete, but we may note certain differences. In the American study the rod and frame were about three times larger than those used in Nigeria (probably subjects made their judgements from a greater distance). In America the tilted body condition was achieved by requiring the subject to stand on a footrest, leaning his body and head against a tilted board, while in Nigeria the subject was seated in a high-backed armchair tilted by wedges placed under the legs, with his feet resting on a footboard, but with his head apparently free to tilt as he wished. Other aspects which may or may not have been equivalent include the order of presentation and the number of trials in each condition. The point of method which is crucial here is that unless the presentation of tasks was controlled exactly across the two groups, any differences in their performance may be due to the tilted body condition being objectively easier in Nigeria and/or the tilted frame condition objectively easier in America.

The most straightforward method of controlling such variables is to use the same apparatus and procedure for all subjects. This is what Beveridge (1939) did in an experiment in Ghana which remarkably foreshadows the Witkin (1959) tilted-room test. His subjects were enclosed in a cupboard through the side of which a straight bar was inserted, and their task was to adjust the bar to true horizontal in total darkness while the whole cupboard was tilted. A group of young African men performed significantly more accurately on this task than a comparison group of somewhat older European men and women. Unfortunately Beveridge did not have the benefit of Witkin's research findings on sex differences, and so failed to control what may have been a critical sampling variable: the European group may have scored less accurately because of the inclusion of women. Here too the evidence is equivocal for the view that West Africans' 'perception is guided less by visual and more by other cues than is that of the European' (Beveridge, 1939:63).

Now that we have examined the 'trees' in some detail, is it possible to discern the overall shape of this 'forest' of cross-cultural research with tests of field-dependency? Witkin and his colleagues have developed a set of standardized tests (even the RFT is now available in a portable version – Morris, 1967) which seem within Western populations to measure a common underlying psychological factor (see *Table 3.1*). How far this factor is an aspect of intelligence, of spatial ability or of cognitive style remains controversial. But individual differences apparently persist over several years (Witkin, Goodenough and Karp, 1967). Moreover these differences seem to be related to aspects of motivation such as social conformity and projective fantasy (Witkin *et al.*, 1962). The origins of these differences in Western populations may well have to do with modes of parental upbringing. Thus Witkin *et al.* (1974) found that children brought up in Holland, Italy or Mexico in villages where the norms place a high premium on obedience to parental authority and discourage children from questioning the prescriptions of authorities, score lower on RFT, EFT and Koh's Blocks than children in the same country raised in villages where the impact of family and social arrangements encourages individuality and independence in children.

Another body of research now exists using various of the tests with African populations. These studies consistently found little or no correlation between performance on the EFT and RFT. It is therefore clear that they do not measure with the same reliability a single underlying factor in these populations. The only exception may be Africans who have experienced prolonged, formal, Western education (Okonji, 1969). Several of these studies find that Western measures of intelligence, number of years at school and the various pictorial tests are all closely correlated (Dawson, 1967; Okonji, 1972; Wober, 1967; Siann, 1972). This suggests that EFT and Koh's Blocks are measuring in this population primarily a cognitive, perceptual factor. There is no direct evidence from Africa for a link between performance on these tests and motivational features of personality.

How could it be that the same tests measure cognitive style in one culture and perceptual skill in another? A useful image

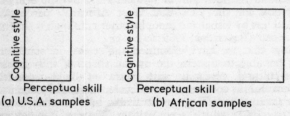

 (a) U.S.A. samples   (b) African samples

Fig. 3.4 *The effect of sampling on the relative contribution of different factors to performance on EFT*

for understanding a comparable issue has been proposed by Colman (1972), who suggested that the question 'which of heredity and environment contributes more to the determination of intelligence?' (see D4) is like the question 'which contributes more to the area of a rectangle, its length or its breadth?' At the general level, both questions are absurd, but in the case of any particular rectangle a valid answer may be given. Let us treat the two sides of the rectangle as cognitive style and perceptual skill and the area as representing performance on EFT. Our question can now be visualized as shown in Fig. 3.4, and as shown there the answer may depend on the particular range of variation present along each dimension in the population we are sampling.

In the USA – where the urban samples studied have experienced a relatively homogeneous physical and educational environment – there will be little variation from one individual to another in the level of perceptual skill required by EFT. Hence any individual differences within this population are more likely to reflect differences in cognitive style than differences in perceptual skill. In African samples (other than highly select, educated groups) the perceptual skills required by EFT will tend to be much more unevenly distributed. For simplicity, I have assumed that the range of variation in cognitive style is the same for the two populations. Thus by comparison with USA studies we should expect to find individual differences in Africa on EFT arising relatively more from differences in perceptual skill. Since the area of the rectangles represents the range of performance on EFT, we may note that another implication of this model is that there will be greater variation in EFT scores in African than in USA samples. Wober's (1967) report suggests that this may well be true for his sample: 'several men failed nearly every item', a maximum of 40 minutes was allowed, 'while the quickest finished the eight items in under four minutes' (1967:34).

Further research will be needed before the issue is settled. But we may note in conclusion a number of general implications for cross-cultural research. Witkin's theory has proved attractive to researchers in this field for several reasons. On the one hand, the emphasis it places on child-rearing and personality links it conceptually to the earlier tradition of cross-cultural research reviewed in Chapter 2. On the other hand, his tests have an objectivity of scoring procedure which seems to bypass some of the problems of interpretation associated with projective tests and interviews. Yet this apparent two-pronged strength may also constitute the theory's essential weakness. The objective record which we make of the subjects' behaviour is strictly confined by these procedures to a situation which outside Western cultures is remote from most of the subjects' previous experience. All the ground-work done by Witkin and his associates in the USA to map out the various factors contributing to performance on these tests needs to be done afresh in each new culture if we are to accept their validity in a new context. Until this is done, studies relating test performance to socialization practices will remain open to a wide variety of interpretations.

The accumulation of studies using these tests does not in itself guarantee that the generality of the theory is enhanced. Yet superficial reviews tend to give this impression. Thus Witkin *et al.* cite as part of a long list of 'evidence from cross-cultural studies', which to them 'suggests, by and large, that the field-dependence–independence phenomenon . . . is to be found in many cultures and is thus not narrowly Western' (1974:13), a study by Siann from which the author herself concluded that 'the concept of field dependency as underlying performance at RFT and EFT may not be particularly relevant in Zambia' (1972:95)!

At the risk of oversimplifying an issue, we may ask ourselves what is the primary goal. Is it to vindicate (with a variety of provisos) a conceptual model developed in the West by showing that it yields results in a variety of different cultures? Or is it to explore, with whatever instruments and models are available, the relation between culture and human behaviour? If the latter is a more important goal, there is a danger in relying too heavily on the theories and more especially on tests established in one cultural context. For it leads too easily to a focus on: 'how do *they* resemble, or differ from, *us*?' rather than the more general question: 'how do different peoples become the way they are?' Wober (1969) has called this the difference between 'centri-cultural' and 'cross-cultural' research. The 'centri-cultural' approach acquires unattractively ethnocentric overtones when the dimension of behaviour investigated is value-laden, as appears to be the case for field-dependency. If theories originally formulated to explain the behaviour of Western populations are to be productive in cross-cultural research they will need to be prised free of particular standardized tests, and new instruments devised appropriate for measuring the same psychological constructs in different cultural settings.

4
The Roles of Language

Language is a very obvious candidate for emphasis as a mediator between culture and behaviour (see A7). Not only is language widely regarded as man's most distinctive behavioural characteristic within the animal kingdom, but it is also a widely recognized distinguishing characteristic for different cultures. 'Certainly, linguistic awareness, linguistic pride, a belief in linguistic specialness and in the inherent untranslatability of one's own vernacular or some other superposed language have been frequent components of the ethnocentrism and the world views of many peoples, past and present' (Fishman, 1960:324). Hence the word used by the ancient Greeks to refer to foreigners, *barbaroi* (from which is derived, with only a slight shift of meaning, the English word *barbarians*), is almost certainly an onomatopoeic attempt to mimic the meaningless sound of their language. A modern parallel seems to exist in the Northern Province of Zambia where Englishmen are sometimes referred to as *aba-yes-yes*! Conversely the notion that English and French have special powers of expression has formed an integral part of the ideologies by which the native speakers of those languages have sought to impose their cultures on the various peoples they have colonized around the world.

Contrastive analysis of languages

Scientific research on the comparison of languages has tended to undermine the supposition that there exists any simple continuum from, say, primitive to sophisticated, or from simple to complex languages. Linguistics commonly subdivides language into three major sub-systems: semantics, syntax and phonology. The first refers to the relations between words and the world to which they refer: it is the main system governing meaning. Syntax is the set of rules by which words are ordered into sentences. And phonology is the sound system which specifies what elementary sounds can be combined to make words and also certain restrictions on how they can be combined (see A7). All languages that have been studied can be shown to possess these abstract, formal properties and not to vary greatly in degree of complexity (Greenberg, 1963).

There are, of course, very considerable qualitative differences of detail across languages. Some illustrations are presented in *Table 4.1* which compares at the three levels English and an African Bantu language, chi-Nyanja. At the semantic level the contrasts are between how the world is segmented by the meanings of single words. The Nyanja word *m'lendo* covers the range of meaning of the English words *stranger* and *visitor*. Conversely the English verb *to wash* covers the meaning of three different Nyanja words. It is a moot point which language can be called more 'powerful' in either situation. The distinction, where it exists, is obligatory: in English it would be anomalous to say 'I am expecting some strangers for lunch,' and in Nyanja it is incorrect to use *ku-capa* for washing your car or your body, or *ku-tsuka* for washing your clothes. In each case we might argue that the language with only one word is deficient in the power to express a conceptual distinction, or we might conversely note the potential of the one-word language to express the link between two concepts with a single multi-faceted word.

The phonological contrasts shown in *Table 4.1* are quite parallel to the semantic ones. English has two sounds which can be used to signal a difference in meaning (i.e., phonemes) /l/ and /r/. In Nyanja, however, although both sounds are heard, no 'minimal pairs' exist like *alive* and *arrive* where only that difference in sound distinguishes between the two words. Conversely in Nyanja the sounds which are represented by the letter p in the English words *spin* and *pin* are distinguished functionally in a way they are not in English. The word *pa* in Nyanja means *at* or *on*, whereas *pha* means *kill*. The only difference in sound between these words is whether the p is released and aspirated (as in the English pin) or not (as in spin): there are no such minimal pairs in English with these sounds, although both occur.

The contrasts in syntax are a bit more subtle. Nyanja is a highly inflected language, so that many additions to the meaning of a verb can be achieved by tacking on various prefixes and suffixes. This achieves a certain economy as shown in *Table 4.1*, where a shift of meaning in English which requires the addition of five new syllables is brought about in Nyanja

Table 4.1 Some qualitative differences between two languages

	English	Nyanja
Semantics	stranger/visitor	m'lendo
	to wash	ku-capa/ku-tsuka/ku-samba
Syntax	a/the	(no articles)
	he comes	a-bwera
	he didn't come back again	s-a-na-bwere-nso
Phonology	alive/arrive	$/l = r/$
		(a single phoneme)
	$/p = p/$	pa/pha
	(a single phoneme)	

with an increase of only two (the hyphens in the Nyanja words are included here only to show their composite structure). Another grammatical difference between these languages lies in the use of the definite and indefinite articles. English requires a decision between *a* and *the* almost every time a noun is used. When the distinction is important, Nyanja takes more words to express it since it has no articles. As we can see in telegrams and newspaper headlines, however, more often than not articles add nothing to the meaning of a sentence: in these cases Nyanja is more economical than English.

Those concepts which play an important part in the life of the community are coded into the language to facilitate communication among adults and transmission of the culture to the young. We can observe this process in the growth of vocabulary in the face of modern technology. It is unimportant from the present perspective whether this is achieved by a systematic recourse to classical root-forms (e.g., *photo-graphy* in most European languages is derived from the ancient Greek for light and drawing), by standardizing a short-hand description (e.g., *kereta api*, the Malay for train, translates literally as *fire-cart*) or by 'borrowing' or adapting a word from another living language (e.g., *fosholo* in Nyanja is an adaptation of the

English word *shovel*). The essential observation is that as a new artefact or process comes within the scope of the culture's need for communication, the language adapts accordingly.

The linguistic relativity hypothesis of Sapir and Whorf

Now some anthropologists have argued that in the transmission of language from one generation to the next there occurs a very fundamental kind of socialization. The child is not merely taught how to use language to express his ideas, he is taught in this process how to think. By the end of this process, 'we see and hear and otherwise experience very largely as we do because the language habits of our community predispose certain choices of interpretation (Sapir, 1929:210). Philosophically this is a very radical assertion, since it undermines the possibility of man's access to the real world. Contrary to the assumptions of many scientists,

> the categories and types that we isolate in the world of phenomena we do not find there because they stare every observer in the face. . . . We cut nature up, organize it into concepts, and describe significances as we do, largely because we are party to an agreement to organize it in this way – an agreement which holds in the pattern of our language. The agreement is, of course, an implicit and unstated one, but its terms are absolutely obligatory; we can not talk at all except by subscribing to the organization and classification of data which the agreement decrees. (Whorf, 1956:212)

At the psychological level this theory of linguistic relativity suggests a very intimate connection between language on the one hand and perception and thought on the other. Such a connection has of course been postulated by psychologists on other grounds. The mystery of how the helpless human infant (literally one who does not speak) develops into an intelligent adult has been attributed to the 'role of language in the regulation of behaviour' (Luria, 1961) or the 'development of verbal mediating processes in children' (Kendler and Kendler, 1962). Others, like Piaget (1954) and Furth (1966), have argued that intelligence is a prerequisite for the symbolic use of language, and that we must therefore look elsewhere to explain the origins of human perception and thought (see A7 and C2). The view that language makes possible new kinds of thought and perception in the child who acquires it is taken one step further by Whorf, who suggests that this advantage is restricted to the particular forms of the specific language he learns.

A great deal of Whorf's writing is concerned with contrasts between various American Indian languages and what he calls 'Standard Average European'. The structural differences which he describes are ingeniously woven into speculations about their implications for thought. Thus:

> in the Hopi language, 'lightning, wave, flame, meteor, puff of smoke, pulsation' are verbs – events of necessarily brief duration must be verbs. . . . The Hopi do not say 'I stayed five days,' but 'I left on the fifth day'. . . . The timeless Hopi verb does not distinguish between present, past and future of the event itself but must always indicate what type of validity the speaker intends the statement to have: (a) report of an event . . . (b) expectation of an event . . . (c) generalization or law about events. . . . Hopi grammar, by means of its forms called aspects and modes, also makes it easy to distinguish among momentary, continued, and repeated occurrences, and to indicate the actual sequence of reported events. . . . The Hopi language has no word really equivalent to our 'speed' or 'rapid'. What translates these terms is usually a word meaning intense or very, accompanying any verb of motion. (1956:215–17)

These features of the language suggest to Whorf that the Hopi people must have an entirely different concept of time from Europeans:

> Hopi may be called a timeless language. It recognizes psychological time, which is much like Bergson's 'duration', but this 'time' is quite unlike the mathematical time, T, used by our physicists. Among the peculiar properties of Hopi time are that it varies with each observer, does not permit of simultaneity, and has zero dimensions: i.e. it cannot be given a number greater than one. (1956:217)

As Fishman has pointed out, this kind of analysis is logically unsatisfactory because 'the very same grammatical designata [features] that are said to have brought about [or merely to reflect] a given *Weltanschauung* [way of looking at the world] are also . . . the only data advanced to prove that such a *Weltanschauung* does indeed exist' (1960:334). What is needed, if we wish to demonstrate that the speakers of a given language not only describe the world in a certain way but actually perceive and think about it that way, is *independent* evidence of their perception or their thought. The study of thinking has always proved an elusive topic, and to approach it without the use of

59

language is especially difficult (see A7). A number of studies, however, have attempted to test Whorf's hypothesis by direct studies of the perception of various language groups.

A classic formulation of predispositions in perception is attentional set. It is well known that the interpretation placed on an ambiguous figure can be biased by giving it a title (Carmichael, Hogan and Walter, 1932; Bruner and Minturn, 1955). Now consider the matching task in Fig. 4.1 (c). The child is required to match the Standard card with whichever of the other two 'it looks most like'. Thus he could choose a card of the same colour or a card with the same word. Because the phonemic distinction l/r is absent from the Nyanja language (see *Table 4.1*) we predicted that, even with English words, Nyanja-speaking children were more likely to treat *glass* and *grass* as equivalent than English-speaking children. And indeed all the English-speaking children who could read matched the words by shape rather than colour, whereas only two out of twenty-six Zambian children who could read did so (Serpell, 1968). This simple experimental result is hardly surprising since printed words and letters are normally coded in terms of their sounds (Conrad, 1964), and the sounds which the letters l and r represent in English are confused by most Zambian primary school children. But what if the contrasts between nonverbal forms are coded linguistically as Whorf suggests? Meaningful shapes like those in Fig. 4.1 (b) are much more often matched in preference to colour than the abstract geometrical shapes in (a). This result has been found for French children (Descoeudres, 1914), Chinese children (Huang, 1945) and Zambian children alike (Serpell, 1966). Is the effect of meaning promoted here by the ease with which children call to mind a distinctive name for each shape?

Carroll and Casagrande (1958) devised a version of this task which was carefully designed to test this notion in a cross-language comparison. One group of American Indian languages, 'the Athapascan languages, employ verb stems that refer . . . to the class of object or objects participating in that event' (Hoijer, 1945). Thus in Navajo it is incorrect to refer to handling such objects as a cigarette and a rope without modifying the stem of the verb. According to the Whorfian hypothesis, speakers of Navajo should therefore perceive the difference between slender, rigid objects and slender, flexible objects as more salient than speakers of English. Carroll and Casagrande (1958) chose their materials so that this kind of distinction formed the basis of one possible match while colour

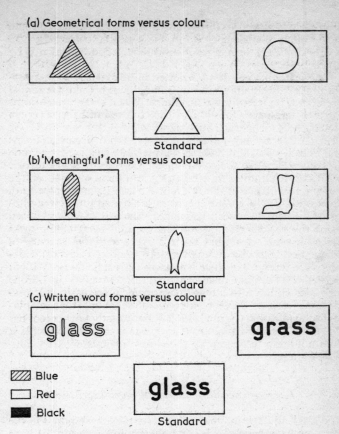

(a) Geometrical forms versus colour

Standard

(b) 'Meaningful' forms versus colour

Standard

(c) Written word forms versus colour

glass   grass

glass
Standard

▨ Blue
▢ Red
■ Black

Fig. 4.1 *The matching-from-sample design*

was the alternative. They found, as predicted, that children who spoke Navajo as their dominant language matched on the verb-stem classified basis more often than their peers from the same reservation whose dominant language was English. However, it seems that among the various influences on attentional set this language factor is at best a rather weak one, since in the same study Boston children of English extraction matched on the verb-stem classified basis even more than the Navajo-dominant, Navajo children! Clearly the Boston children's set to attend to form on this task must be due to some factor other than language, probably perceptual experience. A very similar pattern of results was reported independently by Maclay (1958).

The matching task has been used quite extensively in cross-cultural research and shows up some differences in attentional preference between different groups. When geometrical forms are used in a paper format, African children in Liberia (Irwin *et al.*, 1974) Nigeria (Suchmann, 1966; Kellaghan, 1968), Senegal (Greenfield, Reich and Olver, 1966), Uganda (Evans and Segall, 1969) and Zambia (Serpell, 1969a) all show a much greater preference for colour-matching than is characteristic of Western children at similar ages. When we look at the semantic structure of the relevant African languages we find, however, that the colour spectrum is divided into fewer categories than in European languages. Analysis of how children name the various colours and shapes used in matching tasks makes it quite clear that the relative attentional salience of colour and form for different groups is not a result of 'codability', differences in their languages (Greenfield *et al.*, 1966; Serpell, 1969b). The developmental trend observed in Europe for older children to attend more to form seems from cross-cultural work to be more a result of schooling than of biological maturation (Serpell, 1969a), but exactly how school has this effect remains unclear. If language is at all responsible it does not seem to operate in the simple manner we have considered here.

Language acquisition in multi-lingual societies

The classical issue in cross-cultural psychology is posed in the form we have been considering above: given that individuals A_1 and B_1 *belong* to cultures A and B, how do the differences between *their* cultures account for differences in their behaviour? The italicized words in this formulation reflect a deliberate simplification by which the individual and his culture are said to mutually belong to one another. As we noted in Chapter 1, the number of people who genuinely are affected only by a single cultural tradition has decreased so rapidly in the twentieth century that today they constitute at most a significant minority of the world's population. The 'belonging' conception thus dubs most people as intermediary between cultures, or (in the one-directional view) partly 'acculturated' (often partly 'Westernized'). The dimension of language, however, suggests a different formulation. In the case of the bilingual person the question of which language he belongs to (or belongs to him) is of less interest than how and when he uses each of his options. Rather than construing him as a hybrid composed of two merging cultures, we may conceive of such a person as endowed with a dual repertoire.

In Britain and America bilingualism is seen by many people as a somewhat unusual phenomenon. The adventurous or the gifted pick up a second language at school and thus gain access to the alien worlds of foreign books and foreign countries. But in many, if not most, countries of the world most individuals are expected to be able to operate in at least two different languages. In some cases, like Singapore, several ethnic groups have converged on a major focus of employment. In other cases, arbitrary division by military conquest has demarcated nations which include sections of various ethnic groups (there are many examples in Europe and in Africa). Although the specific details of language use differ from country to country, a useful generalization has emerged from the study of sociolinguistics in the phenomenon of *diglossia*. This refers to a functional separation in society of two languages or dialects (more generally, 'codes'), so that by convention one is used in one type of social situation while the other is reserved for another type. Fishman (1967), who borrowed and extended this concept from Ferguson (1959), notes that across many different countries

> this separation was most often on the lines of an H(igh) language, on the one hand, utilized with religion, education and other aspects of high culture, and an L(ow) language on the other hand, utilized in conjunction with everyday pursuits of hearth, home and work. Ferguson spoke of H and L as superposed languages. (1959:30)

Clearly the L code is what a child first learns at home, and it is on this stage of language acquisition that most of developmental psycholinguistics has concentrated (see C2). Yet when he comes to school, the child has now to learn an H code which may differ in varying degrees from what he has learnt at home. The difficulties faced in this situation by working-class 'black' children in the USA whose home dialect differs somewhat from standard English have recently begun to receive attention. But the order of such difficulties is quite alarmingly increased when radically different languages are used in the

home and the school. It can be argued that it is better to introduce the new language at the very beginning of school, since
the structural differences between the two codes (c.f. *Table
4.1*, p. 57) tend to cause persistent interference for students
who make the transition later in life (Serpell, 1968; Moody,
1973). But the effect of plunging a hitherto monolingual child
into the tasks of learning to read and write in the medium of a
language whose spoken form he has not yet mastered may well
be to postpone his basic literacy by several years (Sharma,
1973). Meanwhile, the H code is reserved for school work, and
the child continues to use the L code as the preferred means of
communication about matters concerning 'hearth and home'.
Thus an estrangement is easily wrought between the culture
of a child's home and what he learns in school. Lemon (1973),
for instance, showed that Tanzanian secondary school students made more clear-cut categorizations and had better integrated constructs in English for a subject taught in that medium
in class, but in Swahili for judgements about people they knew
personally.

Probably the main continuing link between the worlds of
home and school is constituted by the child's peers. Slobin
(1968) has noted that field research among the Koya of
southern India, the Luo of Kenya, the Samoans, and the
'black' Americans of a ghetto in California shows that:

> mothers do not spend much of their time speaking to children
> and that the major input to the language acquisition device
> seems to be the speech of older children. It seems that the
> isolated American middle class home, in which a mother
> spends long stretches of time alone with her children may be
> a relatively rare social situation in the world. (1968:10)

This observation not only raises new questions about the kind
of stimulation required by children to learn their first language,
but also suggests the need for caution in interpreting the studies
by Bernstein (1960) and others of maternal styles of communication with their children in different social classes (see C2,
Ch. 7). It may well be that the early language development, and
indeed much of cognitive development in general, of children
outside Western, middle-class cultures occurs principally in
the context of play with other children.

The relationships which begin at that stage continue in all
probability to provide a major reference group for those students who manage to negotiate the hazards of the highly selective educational pyramid in economically underdeveloped

countries. Thus even at university level, after eight or more years of education in the medium of English, a sample survey of Zambian students showed that about three-quarters of them shared a common Zambian language other than English with their closest friend (Unzapass, 1972). This does not mean, however, that these students always converse with their friends in their first language. Discussions about their studies or about public affairs are more likely to be held in English, the H code, whereas private gossip is more often conducted in a local language. Sometimes a conversation between two people will shift from one code to another and back again. The contextual determinants of such 'code-switching' have been subtly analysed by Gumperz and Hernandez (1971) for Mexican-American bilinguals, by Gumperz and Blom (1971) for dialect variations in Norway, and by Mkilifi (1972) and Parkin (1974) for several languages in Tanzania and Kenya. The choice of code is not simply a matter of which word comes most easily to mind or will be better understood by the speaker's audience. The possible connotations of code-choice include cultural or class snobbery, mockery and social solidarity depending on complex background knowledge shared by the speaker and listeners.

Language in education

The phenomena of diglossia and code-switching by bilinguals illustrate the important fact that a single person can alternate his behaviour between the demands of two or more different cultures. There is no need here to look for an indirect influence of culture through language on thought: speech is in this context the behavioural vehicle of culture in itself. Thus an important part of 'black' American cultural behaviour is speaking in 'Black English', and Kernan has vividly illustrated how it functions 'both as an expression of imposed pariah status and as a complex representation of a cultural system which not only mirrors the former but serves as a refuge from it' (1972:152). It is within such a framework that we can best understand the pressures in various parts of the world for bilingual education in schools:

> Though each area has its own unique set of problems, the need for identity is a common concern. . . . Bilingual education is seen as an agent of social change. In the United States, bilingual education is seen as a way of helping to preserve the

65

identity of American Indians, eventually enabling them to move back and forth between their traditional culture and the main-stream American culture. In the Pacific Islands, bilingual education is seen as a way of reasserting the values of traditional ways of life as a counterbalance to the rapid changes introduced by western contact. In Indonesia, Malaysia, the Philippines and Singapore, bilingual education is seen as a necessary step in establishing a national identity in nations composed of many races and cultures. (Lester, 1974)

Such programmes in most cases give way increasingly to a 'language of wider communication' at the more advanced levels of education, with the result that 'millions of students throughout the world are being taught subjects such as mathematics, history and geography (i.e., subjects other than languages) in the medium of their weaker language' (MacNamara, 1967:121). In many countries the official reasons for this are political and economic: political unity is sought among diverse ethnic groups under the umbrella of a national language, and the availability of instructional materials makes the choice of a Western language economically attractive. There is, however, a more intellectual rationale that has often been advanced, to the effect that 'the native languages have not developed a vocabulary suited to the expression of sophisticated Western concepts and schemata especially in the technological subjects' (MacNamara, 1967:121). This is not necessarily seen as a temporary accident of history, but rather as a consequence of the inherent nature of those languages. Thus Greenfield (1968:1) contends that:

> oral and written speech involve different patterns of language use. . . . Speakers of an oral language rely more on context for the communication of their verbal messages . . . which has important educational correlates as well as implications for cognitive processes. . . . context-dependent speech is tied up with context-dependent thought, which in turn is the opposite of abstract thought.

The details of this theory are based on an analysis of verbal responses by Senegalese and French children when they were asked to explain their choices in a matching task similar to Fig. 4.1b (Greenfield *et al.*, 1966). Two features of the French answers set them apart from those in the Wolof language: superordination and sentential placement. Single words for the concepts 'colour' and 'shape', which are superordinate in a hierarchical sense to terms like red, blue, round, pointed, etc., do not apparently exist in Wolof. But the French terms are assimilated into Wolof especially as it is spoken by educated people. Those children who used such superordinate words included a high proportion of those who were able to shift their matching or sorting responses from one dimension to another. Now this ability to shift the basis of classification has long been interpreted as an index of flexibility and abstract thought (Goldstein and Scheerer, 1941). The relation of verbal superordinate answers to shifting ability was even more marked among French children than among Wolof children.

A second cross-cultural difference in the verbal quality of the answers was grammatical. Monolingual Wolof children more often simply labelled the stimuli as 'yellow' or 'this yellow', whereas children bilingual in Wolof and French (and still more so, monolingual French-speakers) more often embedded the crucial word in a sentence such as 'this is yellow'. Moreover, children who framed their answers in the sentential mode included more of those whose answers identified a common feature shared by the two items which had been matched, and more especially those who did so in a generalized manner (e.g., 'they are both round') rather than an itemized manner (e.g., 'this one is round; this one is round'). Thus Greenfield concludes that the 'French-style education' in Senegalese schools had its effect on children's mode of classification:

at least partly through the training embodied in the written language. Writing is practice in the use of linguistic contexts as independent of immediate reference. Thus, the embedding of a label in a sentence structure indicates that it is less tied to its situational context and more related to its linguistic context. The implications of this fact for manipulability are great: linguistic contexts can be turned upside down more easily than real ones. Once thought is freed from the concrete situation, the way is clear for symbolic manipulation and for Piaget's stage of formal operations in which the real becomes but a subset of the possible. (1968:10)

We will consider in more detail in the next chapter the relevance of Piaget's theory to cognitive development in non-Western cultures. Meanwhile we may note that Greenfield and her associates have raised the linguistic relativity thesis in a new guise when they claim 'to have found an important correspondence between linguistic and conceptual structure' (1966:306).

Heron and Simonsson in a similar vein argue that the best

medium for education is a language which is rooted in a culture that 'places value on concepts and behaviours important for full cognitive development, when "full" implies the goal specified by Piaget' (1969:289). Thus, like Greenfield, they advocate the introduction of education in a foreign culture's language on the grounds that it is better suited to the promotion of cognitive development. It is, however, extremely doubtful whether this argument is grounded in a realistic appraisal of the non-European languages in question. It is only recently that the myth of the 'restricted code' of American 'Black English' has been exploded by the demonstration that this dialect is every bit as elaborate as the Standard English dialect of the dominant culture (Labov, 1969). Two other considerations should make us cautious in accepting the argument. First we know too little as yet about different cultural modes of cognition to be sure in what ways, if any, one is superior to another. And secondly languages are not static.

We noted earlier in this chapter how languages adapt to the impact of technology by expanding their vocabulary. Likewise most of the world's oral languages have now been committed to written form. There is no good reason to suppose that, if it is used in the context of advanced education, *any* language cannot adapt in other more structural ways to the requirements of technology. The issue for developing countries is how to reconcile two formerly independent cultural traditions. One school of thought maintains that the concepts of modern science and technology are inseparably linked to the conceptual structure of Western languages. If this is so, the nation which wishes to 'modernize' must adopt the language along with technology in place of, or at least 'superposed' on, its own traditional languages, abandoning or subjugating the cultural values and identity they enshrine. The alternative implicit in programmes of bilingual education is to give the language of 'hearth and home' an opportunity to expand its range and to act as a bridge between the traditional culture and the demands of the modern world.

5
Cognitive development

The study of cognition (how man acquires knowledge) lies at the centre of several different intellectual traditions. Apart from the theory of linguistic relativity (discussed in Ch. 4) the most popular psychological theory in cross-cultural work on cognition has been Piaget's 'genetic epistemology' (see C2).

> The Piagetian psychologist . . . attempts to describe the basic structures and functioning of higher mental processes. He studies how the child gets to know about his world, how he develops scientific concepts, and how reasoning obeys certain structural properties which can be described by models drawn from logic and mathematics. (Dasen, 1972:23)

This emphasis on the formal, mathematical logic of mental structures is not a mere stylistic device designed to clarify the nature of what has been observed: it reflects the central philosophical theme which has characterized the work of Piaget and his colleagues in Geneva (Flavell, 1963). Thus a group of those colleagues have explicitly contrasted their own 'preoccupation' with 'the regulatory mechanisms underlying the integrative coordination of "information"' against the concern of researchers in the tradition of British and American experimental psychology with 'information-processing techniques' consisting 'of selection, of storage, and of retrieval of relevant cues' (Inhelder, Bovet, Sinclair and Smock, 1966:163).

This contrast exemplifies a major point of controversy in the cross-cultural literature on cognitive development. Some writers have postulated cross-cultural differences in central and pervasive features of the individual's intellect, while others have tried to document the influence of culture on limited and usually relatively peripheral processes. Theories of the central type have suggested reasons why different cultures might promote modes of thinking which lie at different points on the continua of concrete-abstract, magical-rational, emotive-cognitive. Theories of the peripheral type have drawn attention to specific skills and techniques for acquiring or using knowledge, and have shown how different cultures vary in the extent to which they encourage the individual to make use of such devices as aids or tools of thought. Cutting across this dichotomy is another theoretical division between explanations which postulate differences in kind between people of different cultures and those which describe the differences as being a matter of degree (see *Table 5.1*).

The latter, quantitative view, when applied to central, pervasive features of cognition, can be characterized as a theory

Table 5.1 A taxonomy of theories of cross-cultural differences in cognition

	Central pervasive feature e.g. mode of thought	Limited peripheral feature e.g. specific skill
Qualitative difference	'the peculiar properties of Hopi time' (Whorf, 1956)	non-literate Kpelle do not 'learn to provide structures which organize their recall of arbitrary material' (Cole *et al.*, 1971)
Quantitative difference	'retardation in Zulu children of the development of the basic intellectual structures that determine the level of logical thought and abstract reasoning ability' (de Lemos, 1973)	'difficulties in pictorial perception in Africa' (Deregowski, 1968a)

The quotations from particular authors are merely illustrative of a kind of explanation which is proposed quite frequently in the literature. Whorf's approach is discussed in Chapter 4, Cole's and de Lenos' in Chapter 5 and Deregowski's in Chapter 6.

of developmental retardation; whereas a qualitative view of such pervasive differences is illustrated by the Sapir-Whorf theory of linguistic relativity. A quantitative theory of cross-cultural differences in a limited and relatively peripheral process is elaborated in Chapter 6 for the skill of pictorial depth perception. Finally a qualitative view of such limited processes is implied by Cole and his associates in their 'major conclusion that cultural differences in cognition reside more in the situations to which particular cognitive processes are applied than in the existence of a process in one cultural group and its absence in another' (1971:233). As Cole and Bruner (1971) have pointed out, the quantitative views seem to imply a 'deficit interpretation' which often leads to recommendations that the 'deprived' group should be the subject of remedial intervention.

The logic of conservation

One of the dominant features of Piaget's theory is that the qualitative changes with age in the structure of children's thought are characterized by distinctive stages. In the *sensori-motor* stage the infant gradually progresses from simple reflex adjustments to the environment towards an organized system of adaptive behaviour. Next, in the *pre-operational* phase, overt actions begin to be internalized as representations. The resulting concepts, however, are not yet properly integrated into the networks of internally consistent logical thought which Piaget calls cognitive *operations*. The first operations to be mastered are focused on *concrete* objects and events, and permit the classification, ordering, etc., of their physical properties. In the final stage of *formal operations* (which European children begin to reach at adolescence), these are all coordinated within a comprehensive, abstract logic that is applicable not only to the actual world but also to hypothetical propositions. A central feature of the transition from pre-operational to concrete-operational thought is the acquisition of *conservation:* the knowledge that properties such as quantity, weight, and volume remain invariant (i.e. are *conserved*) in the face of various transformations, e.g. when a row of beads is spread out to make a longer line, when a ball of clay is rolled into a snake, or when water is poured from one vessel into another of a different shape. (See C2 for a fuller account of the theory.) 'Implicitly or explicitly, most cross-cultural studies in genetic [i.e.

71

Piagetian] psychology ask whether cognitive development in non-Western cultures follows the same sequential succession of stages as described by Piaget and by many other investigators in middle-class Western children. And if so, do these stages appear at approximately the same age levels?' (Dasen, 1972: 25).

The concrete-operational stage of conservation has been found to be attained by rural Nigerian Tiv children for the concepts of quantity and number (Price-Williams, 1961), and by low s.e.s. urban Chinese children in Hong Kong for area, weight and number concepts (Goodnow, 1962), at very much the same ages as were found for the emergence of these concepts in European children. On the other hand 'a typical curve . . . of "retarded" development has been reported many times, . . . it seems to vary from about one to six years' (Dasen, 1972:28). Dasen's review cites such results from studies of African children in Rhodesia, Senegal and Uganda, Arab children in Algeria and Aden, Eskimo and Indian children in Canada, children of the West Indies, of Iran and Lebanon and also low s.e.s. 'White' children in Europe and Australia. A number of studies of non-Western cultural groups have found only a minority of adolescents giving evidence of conservation, and Dasen cites studies of non-literate adults in rural areas of Australia, Brazil, Ivory Coast, New Guinea, Sardinia and Sicily, finding again many individuals who did not show conservation of one or more concepts.

Studies in this tradition normally employ Piaget's 'clinical method' which requires the tester to try out a variety of probing questions to establish whether a given understanding is present in the individual or not:

Each child is interviewed separately, manipulates the material himself, works at his own rate in an atmosphere of play, and is encouraged to express his ideas to the best of his ability. This seems to the investigator not only the most suitable, but the only possible approach for research with very young children. . . . the investigator has a better opportunity [than with a standardized questionnaire] to assess and increase the cooperation between himself and his child subject, as well as collecting valuable incidental information.

The disadvantage of this method is its lack of precision, controls and exact repeatability, now considered to be almost indispensable in a scientific investigation. (Hyde, 1970:66) (see C1)

To put this last point in a stronger form, we should note the

72

similarity, to which Piaget himself has called attention, between this method and that commonly used in psychiatry. As Farrell (1963) has cogently shown for psychoanalysis, the clinical method of enquiry (to the extent that it allows suggestion) is an extremely unreliable source of evidence about the patient.

Consider, for example, the following excerpt from a study where an Algerian university student is interviewing non-literate rural adult women about conservation of weight:

> in several instances, the initial response was a conservation one. Then when the experimenter, in an attempt to obtain a justification for this response, pointed out the differences in appearance of the two objects, the subjects would no longer give a conservation response. In the course of the dialogue, however, the subjects would return to a conservation judgement, and would be able to relate the various dimensions of the objects by means of a reasoning based on compensation. (Bovet, 1973:324–5)

The author in this case adopts a bias in favour of the more 'mature' response and concludes from these and other data 'that in these adult subjects an underlying logical way of apprehending the problem coexists with an intuitive approach' (1973:325). Yet when seven- to eight-year-old children in this study gave conservation responses to one test and not to another, this led the author 'to doubt the validity of the (children's) statements of invariance of quantity' (1973:318).

The inherent variability of Piaget's clinical method thus makes it a peculiarly unsatisfactory yardstick for comparative studies by different investigators working in different communities. This is not to advocate a rigid adherence to identical procedures for investigating the same process in different cultural groups. Indeed we saw in Chapter 3 good reasons for doubting the validity of such procedures as measures of the same process in different groups. But the adaptation of a test to reveal the operation of 'the same' process in different individuals cannot be done in an *ad hoc* fashion following the researcher's moment by moment intuition. What is called for is systematic variation of the procedures in both the groups to be compared, so as to reveal in a clear manner the complex interaction between subject, test and process.

Fortunately Piaget's methodology includes just this kind of multi-pronged attack on the same hypothetical process. His books are full of ingenious variations on the theme he wishes to study. Not only are there several different tests for a given stage or substage in understanding of a single concept, but the battery is coherently structured in terms of the theory, so that each step in the hypothetical sequence of development is mapped in a strictly parallel fashion for different conceptual areas. Now as Campbell has pointed out:

> if there are multiple indicators which vary in their irrelevant attributes, and if these all agree as to the direction of the difference [between groups] on the theoretically intended aspects, then the number of tenable rival explanations becomes greatly reduced and the confirmation of theory more nearly certain. (1961:345)

One study which claims to have obtained this effect was conducted by Murray (1961) among Zulu and 'white' children in a South African town, each sample comprising two age groups. Every child was given eighteen spatial tests, three of which dealt with topological concepts like order and continuity, eight with concepts in projective geometry like the straightness of lines, and seven with Euclidean concepts like parallelism and distance. On every test at each age level the proportion of 'white' children whose performance was classified as evidence of concrete-operational thought was higher than the corresponding proportion of Zulu children. Thus 'what appears significant [to the author] . . . is the consistency with which the performance of the Zulu children is below that of the white children though a similar sequence of development was present in both groups' (Cowley and Murray, 1962:17). Moreover, 'according to Piaget, the development of spatial concepts is related to the development of the basic intellectual structures that determine the level of logical thought and abstract reasoning ability. A retardation in the development of spatial concepts may therefore indicate a retardation in other areas of mental functioning' (de Lemos, 1973:379). Having interpreted her results as evidence of a quantitative group difference on a central and pervasive feature of cognition (see *Table 5.1*), this author draws the implication that further research should identify deficiencies in the African cultural environment, 'so that modifications could be introduced in the physical, social or educational environment of these children which would help them to achieve the same level of conceptual development as is found in children from Western technological societies' (1973:380).

Not all studies have come to such simple conclusions. Goodnow (1969), reviewing selected studies which used overlapping sets of Piagetian tasks with unschooled 'black' American children, Algerian, Chinese, West Indian, Italian migrant and English children, finds that 'as we move away from a technological society there is not any over-all lag or retardation across tasks, but rather what Vernon . . . has called a series of "peaks and troughs". Some tasks shift their difficulty level more than others' (1969:249). Furthermore, the kind of 'tasks not handled so well outside the traditional [Western, technological] group . . . seem to be predominantly tasks where the child has to transform an event in his head, has to shift or shuffle things around by some kind of visualizing or imaging rather than by carrying out an overt series of changes' (1969: 249). Now this spatial-perceptual ability to perform 'imaged transformations' is intimately involved in Piaget's account of concrete-operational thought about space. Thus the apparent variety of Murray's tests we considered above may be confined within a critical narrow range of mental processes that are favoured by Western culture. Not only does this evidence call into question the validity of Murray's inferences about general retardation, but it also links up with the evidence we presented in Chapter 3 concerning the skills required to obtain high scores on tests of field-independence. We will come across yet more evidence of cross-cultural differences in this highly specific perceptual skill in Chapter 6, when we consider pictorial tasks involving the orientation of abstract geometrical shapes.

The failure of concrete-operational thought to emerge for all different concepts at once is not a 'discovery' of cross-cultural work. Piaget recognized this phenomenon and called it 'horizontal décalage', that is the 'temporal displacement' or 'uncoupling' from its conceptual partners of a formative pattern relative to the overall theory of developmental sequence. The significance of 'décalages' has been described by Flavell as one of the limitations of concrete-operational thought.

> The concrete-operational child . . . has to vanquish the various physical properties of objects and events (mass, weight, length, time, area, etc.) one by one because his cognitive instruments are insufficiently 'formal', insufficiently detached and dissociated from the subject matter they bear upon, to permit content-free once-for-all structuring. (1963:204)

We see here both the weakness and the strength of Piaget's theory. 'Task contents do differ in the extent to which they resist and inhibit the application of cognitive structures' (1963: 23). To the extent that such resistance varies according to experience it ceases to be meaningful to try and locate an individual on the continuum of development for Piaget's global stages. But, by identifying this phenomenon, a systematic way is opened up for studying the effects of experience on the development of cognitive skills.

Price-Williams, Gordon and Ramirez (1969) took up this opportunity by comparing children of Mexican families which specialized in pottery-making with children of the same community who lacked this particular opportunity to manipulate clay. In one location the potters' children were significantly more advanced in the test with clay of conservation of substance, but the groups did not differ reliably on other conservation tasks relating to the concepts of number, liquid, weight and volume where other materials were used. In a second location following the same research design, they found the potters' children to be markedly superior on all five of the conservation tasks. Their results are thus inconclusive. In one case it appeared that the logic of conservation was mastered only in the context of a specific, practised skill, while in the other case the experience in one medium seems to have had a generalized effect on cognitive development (unless, of course, the samples in the second study differed in some other, uncontrolled respects).

It should be noted that, in order to test for such specific effects, broad categories of skill such as 'numerical', 'spatial' or 'temporal' are not precise enough. Thus Dasen, who found inconsistent evidence about the relation of spatial development to Aboriginal culture in Australia, points out that:

> the spatial concepts . . . we are studying are only partly equivalent to those needed for survival by Aborigines . . . whereas they are the spatial concepts typically relevant to the European culture. It would be interesting to analyze, in less general terms than we have done here, the spatial skills and concepts actually required by nomadic people, and to construct tests accordingly. (1973:406)

One feature of the cross-cultural results obtained with Piaget's tests which is often emphasized is the universality with which children of different ages seem to 'proceed' through the qualitative stages identified by the theory. Moreover, it is common to find authors noting with surprise the qualitative similarity of their protocols to those reported from Geneva. Thus Hyde writes:

> it was a common experience to hear a small Arab, Somali or

Indian child give in Arabic almost a word for word translation of an answer given to the same question by a Swiss child. . . . Not only verbal answers, but the types of mistakes they make in the practical problems followed those of the Swiss subjects very closely. (1970:197)

Should we interpret such qualitative similarities as evidence that an adult in New Guinea, for instance (Prince, 1968), has the same command of logic as a six-year-old Swiss child? In my view we need to be more specific, and say that both individuals apply the same logic in the particular set-up devised by Piaget. This convergence in behaviour may be more a consequence of the limitations imposed by the task than of similarities in the overall structure of their intellects.

One study, however, has suggested that even within the constraints imposed by the conservation tests, 'different modes of thought can lead to the same results' (Greenfield, 1966:254). The experiment begins with the child equalizing the amount of water contained in two identical beakers, A and B. Next the water from A is poured into a third beaker, C, which is taller and thinner than the others, so that the water level rises. The child is now asked whether C contains more or less water than B. Those of her unschooled rural Wolof subjects in Senegal who showed that they had mastered conservation on this task, explained their judgements in ways that suggested they had reached this understanding by a different route from that followed by Western-educated children. School-educated children master the problem by establishing a concept of present identity which is firmly distinguished from the equivalence of appearances. 'The Wolof children, by contrast, achieve conservation by establishing identity between the *successive* states of past and present. Their link might be either the continuity of action from one part of the experiment to another, or the constant appearance of the standard beakers' (1966:255).

Additional evidence to support this view is provided by a comparison of two methods of modifying the test. One procedure involved screening the perceptual cues which seem to mislead young American children into giving non-conservation responses (Bruner, 1966). This method improved the scores of urban Wolof schoolchildren but was of little help to the unschooled rural subjects. Another method, however, did help this group much more, and this was to allow the subject to pour the liquid himself instead of watching the experimenter do so. This pouring method conversely was of no help to urban schoolchildren. Greenfield's explanation postulates a belief on the part of the traditionally oriented rural children that the action of pouring by the experimenter is responsible for a change in the quantity of the water. This kind of belief in 'action magic' is suppressed, she suggests, by Western education.

Now the specific form of Greenfield's interpretation is open to a number of possible criticisms. The screening and pouring methods differ in a number of respects, any one of which might be responsible for the effect. Bovet (1973), for instance, has pointed out that when engaged in the act of pouring a child may attend to different stages of the procedure from those which are salient to a passive observer. Moreover, no evidence of a cultural tradition has been adduced to support the idea that teenage Wolof children could really be expected to see magic in the pouring of water by an experimenter. Nevertheless, Greenfield's attempt to sort out by experimental means the exact cognitive basis for success or failure on the conservation test by different groups of subjects represents an important advance on most other cross-cultural Piagetian research. Bryant (1974) has shown in a series of experiments that much of the difficulty experienced by young English children with Piaget's tests of conservation arises from the particular form those tests take. And his refined observations suggest an alternative interpretation of their 'deficit' more related to limited perceptual strategies than to central cognitive structures. If the various component skills which contribute to performance can be systematically related to environmental variables, not only will Piaget's theory be productively elaborated but this field of research may become easier to relate to other lines of cross-cultural work. A preliminary attempt has been made by Furby (1971).

Conceptual organization

When a child is asked to sort a collection of items into those which belong together, he performs at the perceptual level the same kind of matching task which we described in Chapter 4 (see Fig. 4.1). In Piaget's terminology, however, the child is doing something more complex, namely conceptual classification. It is interesting to note, therefore, that just as the introduction of familiar shapes increases the likelihood in the matching task of responding to form, so the use of familiar materials in the sorting task increases the abstractness of classification. Thus Okonji (1971) found that Nigerian eleven- to twelve-year-old children used more superordinate concepts (see p. 66) to justify their sorting of items than Scottish children of the same age when the materials consisted of objects commonly found in Nigeria but seldom seen in Scotland. The same trend was apparent but statistically unreliable among six- to ten-year-old children. On the other hand, when miniature models of animals were used, which both groups could be expected to recognize, there was no significant difference on this measure between the groups, with the Scots scoring marginally higher at the younger age levels.

Another study held the content of the materials to be sorted constant, but varied the form in which they were presented (Deregowski and Serpell, 1971). In this case the measure of performance was the number of categories into which the subject sorted the items. When miniature models of animals and motor vehicles were used, young Scottish children and Zambian children matched for education obtained similar scores. But when the task was to sort photographs of the same models, the Scottish children obtained higher scores irrespective of whether the photographs were coloured or not. A similar reduction in classification skill was found by Sigel, Anderson and Shapiro (1966), by using pictures instead of objects with low s.e.s., but not with middle-class, 'black' American children. We will look in greater detail at cultural differences in pictorial perception in Chapter 6.

These demonstrations of how familiarity with the form and content of materials to be sorted can affect the degree of 'abstraction' shown in children's reponses are ample justification for the decision by Price-Williams (1962) to confine his study of classification in a rural Nigerian community to materials drawn from the local environment. His finding that the level of abstraction attained was lower in the case of animals than in the sorting of leaves may well reflect the fact that the animals presented were, of course, toy models, whereas in the case of leaves no perceptual effort was required to identify the objects to be sorted, since actual leaves were used.

One of the most useful functions of conceptual organization is to reduce the information load on memory (see A6). Bartlett's (1932) classical study of remembering showed how stories and pictures are reproduced, by English adults, around a schema which holds together the various details so that the latter are often distorted to fit in more coherently with the meaning the subject has read into the overall theme. Likewise Miller (1956) showed that the limit on the number of arbitrary items, like digits, that a person can retain in short-term memory can be greatly extended if he learns to code the items into larger 'chunks' from which the details can later be retrieved. Such techniques are often used by 'mnemonists' to achieve their impressive feats of memory (Hunter, 1964).

In studies of memory using the test procedure of free recall, the subject is presented with a random string of words or objects and, after a given interval, asked to repeat back the words in any order he likes. Much interest has centred on whether items in the list are recalled in clusters which are related by some conceptual similarity. Not surprisingly it appears that subjects who employ the strategy of clustering are able to recall a larger number of items than those who recall in a random order. Just as with the sorting task, it can be argued that in clustering, 'the classification is a hierarchical mental process; the subject notes common conceptual properties among various items, which permits classification into superordinate categories' (Jensen and Frederiksen, 1970:104). Since this is an example of what Jensen terms Level II ability, 'characterized by transformation and manipulation of the stimulus prior to making the response' (1970:4), these authors conclude that the difference they observed in the extent of clustering between low s.e.s. 'black' and upper middle-class 'white' American, fourth grade schoolchildren is a reflection of different levels of intelligence in the two groups.

A series of studies with this kind of procedure has been conducted in Liberia with Kpelle children and adults, some of whom have attended Western schools while others have not (Cole *et al.*, 1971, Ch. 4). In the classic situation subjects with little or no formal education gave no evidence of clustering and showed rather poor recall. On the other hand, when the items to be recalled were embedded in a story which structured them into clusters, recall was highly clustered. A number of variations in procedure were explored in order to investigate the source of difficulty in the standard test situation. Arranging the order of presentation in blocks of conceptually clustered items promotes more clustering for both educated and non-literate subjects. But merely announcing the names of categories into which a random list could be clustered (whether at the time of presentation, at the time of recall, or both) was of negligible assistance to Kpelle primary schoolchildren, although work with American subjects had found this facilitated clustering and recall. Only if the Kpelle subject was guided by requiring him to recall all the members of each category in succession did clustering occur and then it greatly assisted recall. In some conditions, however, these subjects used a structure without prompting at recall. Thus if the objects belonging to a given category were held up, whenever they occurred in the random sequence, over a particular chair (in a row of four chairs between the subject and experimenter), recall by Kpelle schoolchildren was highly clustered and greatly increased over a control condition where the items over a given chair did not belong to a single category. Similarly Scribner found that if non-literate rural Kpelle adults were required to sort a collection of objects and to repeat their preferred system of sorting, recall of the objects (once removed) was clustered according to their own grouping (Cole and Scribner, 1974, Ch. 6).

These experimental variations produce such up-and-down results that it seems we are probably dealing with context-specific skills. The transformation of the stimulus, which Jensen sees as a sign of higher-level intelligence, seems to occur for different groups under different conditions. It is true that those variations which induce clustering in Kpelle subjects seem to provide guidance at least at the time of 'input'. But as Herriot (1973) has argued, such guidance surely 'benefits the subject because it allows him to exercise a function he actually possesses. In this case *any* beneficial effect is to be treated as evidence of ability . . . A real absence of function is indicated by inability to benefit by these or any other cues' (1973:160). What might be the origin of cross-cultural differences in the cues which are effective in inducing subjects to apply conceptual organization to a memory task? Cole and Scribner imply that they may arise from the intimate link between school experience and the testing situation:

In the course of normal events, things are remembered because their natural contexts are organized in ways that matter to the individual and make sense in terms of his social experiences . . . Unlike most common memory situations, our experimental version of free recall uses material that is not connected grammatically. The items named are familiar, but the motivation to remember them comes from an arbitrary source, such as the desire to earn money or appear clever. . . There is little doubt that success in school, among other things, requires of children that they learn to commit large amounts of intitially unrelated material to memory. (1974:139)

Moving still further away from the 'epistemological' perspective of Piaget, concept formation has been studied under a set of procedural conditions modelled on the behaviourist methods for studying animal learning (see A3). When a subject learns to respond to one of a pair of stimuli consistently over a series of trials he can be said to have mastered a discrimination or to have identified a concept. The precise nature of the cognitive change which underlies his behaviour can be inferred by comparing his performance when the problem is changed in various ways. One kind of change which has received particular attention is the relative length of time taken to master two different problems one after the other. The study of such 'concept shifts' forms the bulk of the evidence for Kendler and Kendler's (1962) verbal mediation theory of developmental changes in concept formation (see C2, Figs. 2.1 and 2.2) and for Harlow's (1959) theory of learning set. Cole and his associates have used this research design in another series of experiments with Kpelle subjects in Liberia. These methods were 'not chosen as representative of common Kpelle problem-solving situations, but rather as possibly useful special situations in which the general processes underlying problem-solving and concept formation could be manifested clearly enough to permit detailed analysis' (1971:146).

We do not have the space here to examine the details of all their experiments, but we will note the authors' conclusions and some general guidelines for interpreting these and other studies along the same lines. The authors believe they 'can now identify with some confidence the learning mechanisms that underlie' certain of their 'results'.

> The improvement associated with a series of problems having a single principle of solution occurs only if subjects learn in what we have called a dimension-based manner. This dimension-based (concept-based would be an acceptable alternative term) learning, in turn, requires that the subject respond to sub-problems as instances of a general problem, rather than learning each sub-problem in isolation. . . . In identifying a pattern of learning that treats each sub-problem as an isolated unit, we seem to have stumbled upon an example of what is ordinarily termed rote learning. (1971:175)

They then proceed to suggest, as with 'clustering' (see above, p. 80), that cultural differences reside in the situations in which the process of dimension-based learning will be brought to bear on a problem.

The first thing to note about these conclusions is that they postulate a qualitative difference, albeit situation-bound, in 'the general learning processes underlying . . . concept formation' (see *Table 5.1*). Now this is very controversial. For instance, the extensive literature on relatively stable attentional preferences for certain dimensions over others (e.g. the bias in favour of colour by African children reviewed in Ch. 4) 'suggest(s) that almost all subjects, regardless of age, tend to dimensionalize the stimuli at the outset of the concept shift task' (Wolff, 1967:396). A number of different processes seem to be involved in determining the ease with which a child carries over what he has learned in one problem to the next, and these interact in different ways with the particular details of the task (Slamecka, 1968). Consider, in particular the reversal shift, a task which requires the subject to shift to choosing the opposite value of the same dimension (e.g. from white shapes to black shapes). This was used extensively by the Kendlers, and by Cole and others in Liberia, and is subject to a variety of higher-order strategies quite separate from the issue of dimensional control (Gollin, 1965; Trabasso, Deutsch and Gelman, 1966). It is quite likely, therefore, that closer analysis would show that the differences between non-literate Kpelle and Western-educated children on these tasks arise from a variety of specific interactions between the structure of the stimuli and different 'hierarchies of cue-utilization strategies and cue salience' (Jeffrey, 1968:324) in the two populations.

A more general issue concerning this research is raised by the authors themselves, who note that 'the American emphasis on classification according to physical attributes, such as color and form, and the dependence of (their) research techniques on pictorial representation and non-meaningful stimuli play directly to an area of experience almost wholly lacking among the Kpelle' (Cole *et al.*, 1971:145). By accepting this emphasis, these authors have in this instance failed to keep separate the guiding principles of research strategy and the detailed tactics of its implementation. There are many features of the experimental paradigm used in discrimination learning studies which are essentially marginal to the theories the authors seek to test. Most experiments present small geometrical figures, which the subject must respond to by pressing a button or lever, against a background of silence in a room with blank walls, and with feedback confined to isolated words of praise or automatically delivered sweets. Yet any one of these characteristics can demonstrably be waived without a loss of theoretical interest to the study (Serpell, 1973). Indeed, if the theory is to be seen to have relevance to everyday life these artificial restrictions must eventually be abandoned. In cross-cultural work the problem is doubly serious, since the 'simplifications' which are accepted by Western subjects as natural features of a scientific laboratory may well be so perplexing to subjects in other cultures as to seriously modify their behaviour.

Cognitive strategies

One way of resolving the controversy outlined in *Table 5.1* (see p. 70) is to break down a complex behaviour into its components. A qualitative change in the central 'regulatory mechanisms underlying . . . integrative coordination' (Inhelder *et al.*, 1966) might turn out to be reanalysable as the sum of a number of quantitative changes in specific 'information-processing techniques'. In the Kpelle studies of concept shift, for instance, one result which lends itself to this approach is concerned with 'spontaneous reversal'. The task in question requires the subject in fact to learn two 2-choice discriminations (e.g., a red cross must be chosen in preference to a black cross, and a grey square in preference to a grey triangle) concurrently on randomly alternating trials . What happens when the solution to one problem is reversed (e.g. choice of the black cross is now rewarded)? Some subjects (especially older schoolchildren) immediately conclude that the other problem will also be reversed (i.e. they choose the grey triangle at the next opportunity), while others don't. Cole and his associates interpret this as evidence of the degree to which the subject 'treats each subproblem as an isolated unit', a case of 'rote learning'. But an equally plausible account of the data they present is that the older schoolchildren's behaviour involves 'the operation of a response rule to shift in the face of non-reinforcement for the previously correct response' (Trabasso, Deutsch and Gelman, 1966:19). This kind of guesswork is often observed in the behaviour of Western college students on such tasks and can even interfere with their learning when the solution is a very simple one (Stevenson, Iscoe and McConnell, 1955).

Strategies can also play an important role in performance on memory tasks. Scribner actively encouraged her subjects to make use of such strategies in a study with high-school and non-literate villagers in Liberia. Before they began a two-minute period of memorizing twenty-four familiar objects, they were instructed either to 'do anything you want to help you remember' or, more specifically, to carry the objects to another table 'in any way that will help you remember'. Since the objects could be classified into a number of obvious categories, she expected that subjects would group them in order to remember them in clusters. Hardly any subjects in either group did so in the first condition, but half of the high-schoolers did engage in some grouping activities in response to the carrying instructions. Interestingly, 'although the villagers failed to regroup the material, they did engage in other memorizing techniques – almost all named the items and rehearsed the names during the study period; some demonstrated and described the functions of the items as well' (Cole and Scribner, 1974:137).

Kingsley (1974) examined the same issue under different task conditions. The basic situation was designed to be familiar to his young urban Zambian subjects: a motherly Zambian experimenter sent the child to fetch six items from an array of twenty familiar objects which they had examined together a little earlier in a neighbouring room. But before the child set off he was left alone to wait for sixty seconds in a room where the experimenter had examined with him a set of photographs of the objects. The subject 'was told that he could use anything in the room to help him remember; a pencil and some bits of paper lay prominently on the table in front of the child in addition to the photographs' (1974:9). An observer watching through a one-way screen recorded the child's behaviour while he waited. Seven- to ten-year-old schoolchildren remembered better on this task than children of the same age living in the same low s.e.s. district who were not attending school. Their strategies, however, seem to have been largely confined to rehearsal. More lip movements were observed in the school-children than the non-schoolers. Hardly any children wrote anything on the paper or carried along the photographs which the experimenter had pointed to when specifying what they should fetch, perhaps 'because writing skill itself is so little developed in these children at this age' and because they failed 'to understand that it would actually be permitted to take the photographs along'. About one-third of all the children 'did pick up the photographs or sort through them during the delay interval, but without actually taking them along' (1974: 10–11).

To carry along the photographs or to write down a 'shopping

list' might appear in a sense to be cheating in a memory task. And yet these are merely more visible and formal aids with the same purpose as clustering and rehearsal. By reducing the load on the intellect they serve as tools which increase the individual's capacity. Bruner and his associates have developed the idea proposed by Lévi-Strauss (1963) that every culture accumulates a stock of 'amplifying tools' – 'images, skills, conceptions, and the rest' (Bruner, 1966).

> By an amplifying tool is meant a technological feature, be it soft or hard, [in the language of computers] that permits control by the individual of resources, prestige, and deference within the culture. An example of a middle-class cultural amplifier that operates to increase the thought processes of those who employ it is the discipline loosely referred to as 'mathematics'. To employ mathematical techniques requires the cultivation of certain skills of reasoning, even certain styles of deploying one's thought processes. If one were able to cultivate the strategies and styles relevant to the employment of mathematics, then that range of technology is open to one's use. If one does not cultivate mathematical skills, the result is 'functional incompetence', and inability to use this kind of technology. (Cole and Bruner, 1971:872)

Kingsley (1974) examined the impact of Western-style schooling on the early stages of acquisition of mathematical reasoning. The most elementary strategy in this field is that of counting. Kingsley found that among the same Zambian children described above, seven- to eight-year-old schoolchildren can 'count up to 10' in rote fashion better than their peers not in school, although nine- to ten-year-olds could almost all do so whether or not they were attending school. When, however, they were given the task of estimating the number of bricks in variously shaped constructions made of six to thirteen bricks, schoolchildren, about as often as non-schoolers, merely inspected the model rather than applying their numerical knowledge. The schoolchildren were likewise no more systematic than their unschooled peers in estimating the relative quantities of larger numbers of beads in a series of different-sized jars. Thus he concludes that in this population:

> schools do teach quantitative mediating skills like counting (although some of these are eventually learned without schooling also), but when it is a question of inducing a disposition to use available quantitative mediating strategies, schools appear to do little better than everyday life. (1974:17)

The nature of mathematical thinking in a non-Western culture has been further explored by Gay and Cole (1967).

We have moved in this chapter from a consideration of theories which attempt to relate the overall organization of thought with cultural factors, to a more modest analysis of specific cognitive strategies in the context of particular tasks and their relation to past experience. One justification for this shift of emphasis was suggested above, namely that apparent cross-cultural differences in the quality of generalized features of cognition may turn out to be nothing more than the cumulative effect of a number of quantitative differences on lower-level dimensions of behaviour. An additional reason for the experimental psychologist to favour this reductionist approach is that it lends itself to more precise definitions and controls in the design of studies to test the theory against the facts. In the experimental analysis of human skills, modern research 'places the main emphasis on perception and decision' (Welford, 1968:196). It is therefore not too surprising that we find in the realm of perception some of the most precise theorizing in cross-cultural psychology. In the next chapter we will consider how much light it can throw on the difficult subject of culture and cognitive development.

6
Pictorial perception

We have already seen in previous chapters several instances in which the perceptual impact of pictures seems to differ across cultures. In Chapter 3 the possibility was considered that cross-cultural differences in response to EFT reflect differing levels of perceptual skill in the task of locating items embedded in a picture. And in Chapter 4 we concluded that cross-cultural differences in attention to colour and shape often arise from differences in familiarity with the geometrical forms which predominate in modern Western pictorial designs. But in each of these cases a rival school of thought exists, which treats the pictorial aspect of the tasks as incidental to the main topic of investigation. The notion that the pictorial medium of presentation in itself may affect the performance of different cultural groups in different ways comes from a separate tradition of research on pictures in their own right.

A growing body of evidence now exists that pictures drawn according to modern, Western conventions do not evoke the same kind of response in people of different cultures (notably in Africa) as they do in Western, formally educated populations (Hudson, 1967). As usual, a variety of alternative explanations have been proposed. (1) Perhaps the most remote from pictorial perception itself is the suggestion that responses may differ because the questions asked about the picture have not been clearly phrased. Evidently if the artist's intention is not understood by the subject, we are dealing with a failure of communication. But is this due to a misperception of the picture or to a failure to understand the task? (2) Another very general issue is posed by Wober's (1966) theory of sensotypes (see Ch. 3). Are pictures poorly understood because they rely exclusively on the visual modality, whereas in certain non-Western cultures other sensory modalities receive greater emphasis? (3) One of the most pronounced areas of difficulty in interpreting Western pictures for many African samples has been the representation of distance or depth in the third dimension. Some writers have hinted at an ecological explanation for this in terms of impoverished distance perception in the real world as a result of living in a densely forested environment where long distances are seldom viewed.

1 Communication difficulties extraneous to the picture

In any investigation on pictorial perception, there is always the difficulty in asking questions about the pictures, that some of the children will answer in terms of the actual drawings whereas some will accept the questions as referring to the persons or objects *represented* by the drawings. (Duncan, Gourlay and Hudson, 1973:83)

Thus if we were to ask a child which animal is larger in Fig. 6.1, the elephant or the antelope, a choice of either animal would be a legitimate answer: the drawing of the elephant is the smaller of the two, but of course it represents a larger animal than the antelope. This argument was taken up by Miller (1973) in relation to the spatial relations among the items. Fig. 6.1 is one of a series of drawings designed by Hudson (1960) to be ambiguous with regard to the question: 'Which is nearer the man, elephant or antelope?' And in his original research with these drawings he interpreted his subjects' answers to this question as evidence of how they perceived pictures. Various samples, which he prefers to call 'unacculturated' (including young 'white' South African children, 'black' Africans with varying degrees of education and isolated 'white' forest workers), more often gave the two-dimensional (2-D) answer than Western, educated samples.

Miller, however, argues that

it is entirely possible that a viewer . . . could perceive the elephant as being represented as further away but still interpret the question literally. The reality of the situation was that the elephant, as measured on the flat piece of paper, was drawn closer to the man, and if the subject interpreted the instructions

89

literally, he would so respond, even if he were capable of
perceiving the third dimension. (1973:142)

As Wittgenstein (1958) pointed out, however, the meaning of
a statement (or question) is best understood in terms of the
rules of the 'language game' which apply to the context in
which it was uttered. And as Olson (1970) has shown, these
semantic rules are partly determined, not only by the words,
but by the perceived structure of the environment to which the
words refer. The context leading up to Hudson's controversial
question is as follows. First the subject is asked to identify the
items represented: man, spear, elephant, tree, hill, antelope.

Fig. 6.1 *One of Hudson's (1960) ambiguous drawings to test
the perception of depth in pictures*

Next he is asked 'What is the man doing?' And 'if a candidate
reported that the man was aiming or throwing the spear without specifying his quarry, an additional question was asked to
clarify whether he was aiming at elephant or antelope' (Hudson,
1960: 189).

Thus before a subject answers the question about spatial
relationships on this test, he has identified the man as a hunter
engaged in the act of throwing a spear. To the Western, educated observer this makes it very clear that a question about
who is nearer to whom refers to the animals and person represented and not to the pattern of lines on the surface of the
paper. And indeed the author notes that 'candidates in all

samples, choosing the elephant as the hunter's quarry, were those who perceived the elephant as nearer the hunter than the antelope' (1960:203). Now whether we regard the basis of this interpretation of the picture as being perceptual or semantic, it seems clear that the ambiguity of the test lies not in the wording of the question but in the structure of the picture. Mundy-Castle (1966) provides further evidence of the real-world nature of his Ghanaian subjects' interpretations of Fig. 6.1, with details of their replies to questions such as 'Can the man see the antelope?'

A different line of argument was advanced by Omari and Cook (1972). Several investigations with young children have found that the phrasing of questions about relational concepts (e.g. 'bigger than') tends to be difficult. How much of this difficulty arises from a cognitive attitude marked by egocentricity (Piaget and Inhelder, 1956) and how much from an incomplete mastery of adult vocabulary (Donaldson and Wales, 1970) is unclear (see C2, and Bryant, 1974). But it seemed possible that different wordings of Hudson's crucial question might afford different cognitive cues to the spatial relations involved. They conducted an experiment with third-grade New York children ('Blacks' and Puerto Picans) in which three parts of the question 'Which is nearer the man?' were varied: 'man' or 'you'; 'is' or 'looks'; and 'nearer' or 'farther'. Only the last of these had any effect on the pattern of children's responses, 'farther' yielding more 3-D replies than 'nearer'. The authors suggest two possible explanations for this effect: the word 'farther' may be easier to understand since it is the 'unmarked' (or more basic) member of the pair of concepts farther-nearer (see A7, C2); or it 'might have a directive or attentional function, facilitating the Ss focusing on the inverse relationship of changing size with distance' (Omari and Cook, 1972:323). Since, however, all the pictures they used show the elephant in the far distance, their results could equally well be due to a preference by the children for answering 'elephant', perhaps because it was mentioned first. Kingsley, Allison and Noble (unpublished) failed to replicate these results with sixth-grade Zambian children. Page (1970) found a dramatic increase in 3-D responses to one of Hudson's (1960) drawings when he asked which animal was nearer to the observer (you). But since this question followed the standard question with an emphatic stress on 'you', it may have biased the replies towards a change.

We have probably not exhausted the range of objections that could be raised about Hudson's questioning procedure.

For instance, the equivalence of terminology might be questioned when the text is translated into other languages. The weight of the available evidence, however, is against dismissing Hudson's results as artefacts arising from failure to communicate the task. People in most of the samples tested identify the individual items in the pictures with little difficulty. Moreover as we shall see below, the specific failure of certain groups to interpret the spatial relationships in 3-D has been demonstrated with other pictures, using quite different questions (Duncan *et al.*, 1973: 122) and even with non-verbal test procedures (Deregowski, 1968a, 1969a; see Fig. 6.3).

2 *Dominance of the visual modality*

One of the samples which failed to interpret Hudson's (1960) pictures as three-dimensional was composed of adults from a very isolated 'white' community in South Africa. These people are descended from a population which entered the region of the Knysna forest in the early nineteenth century and has experienced very limited contact with the outside world since then (Mundy-Castle and Nelson, 1962). Apparently referring to this group, who represent a limited gene pool, Hudson wrote:

> It may well be that the physical environment promoted auditory perceptual development at the expense of visual perception. In the bush and the forest, the ear was a better predictor of danger than the eye, and so by a process of natural selection auditory perceptual organization became more characteristic of their culture than visual perceptual development. One aspect of such cultural qualitative differences might lie at a superficial level of perceptual organization viz. depth perception of pictorial material. (1960:206–7)

Clearly one implication of this analysis is that most visual skills should be somewhat depressed, and by contrast auditory skills should be enhanced, in this population. This same hypothesis was in fact advanced by Biesheuvel (1943) without the genetic emphasis, in discussing the relatively poor performance of Africans on visual, Western tests. As we saw in Chapter 3 it has also been elaborated by Wober (1966) under the heading of 'sensotypes'. The important feature to note about this theory in the present context is that it is relatively undiscriminating: pictorial depth perception is treated as merely one of a great range of visual skills which are favoured by the Western sensotype and less favoured by the African sensotype. We now know that certain limits can be set to such a generalization. Poortinga (1971) tested under laboratory conditions the visual and auditory acuity of educated, adult 'white' and 'black' South Africans and found no reliable group differences in either modality. However, since these tasks were at a very simple sensory level Biesheuvel has questioned their relevance to his hypothesis, which is concerned with the higher mental processes involved in perception, communication, and reasoning. It may still be true, he argues, that these are more readily performed by Africans in the auditory modality even though their sensory capacities are not biased in that direction (Poortinga, 1971:76).

A more elaborate study of the sensotype hypothesis was undertaken with Zambian and English schoolchildren (Serpell, 1974). We looked at their performance on a series of copying tasks in various media. One test which required no apparatus at all consisted of imitating with one's own hands a given arrangement of fingers displayed by the tester. Some children did this test blindfold by feeling the tester's hands. There was no difference in accuracy between eight-year-olds in Lusaka, Zambia and in Manchester, England on this task, both groups scoring much lower without vision than with their eyes open. Another set of tasks which were performed with or without vision involved reproducing models of various shapes, either in the medium of plasticine or by bending thin strips of wire. The latter is a game widely played by Zambian boys, who like building toy cars in this way, and we were not surprised to find that they scored much higher on this test than English boys. Plasticine modelling was roughly equivalent across the groups, the Zambian children probably having acquired the necessary skill by moulding earthen clay. Both groups were very much disoriented in these modelling tasks by loss of vision, and although the Zambian boys maintained their superiority there was no evidence that it was greater under these conditions than with vision. Contrary to sensotype theory, wire-modelling appears to be a specifically African skill which is primarily guided by visual cues.

Finally we should note that when children in the same two populations were asked to copy the same shapes with a pencil on paper, the order of abilities was reversed. English children were now much more accurate than Zambian children. All these copying tasks were performed better by twelve-year-old, Grade 6 Zambian children than by eight-year-olds in Grade 2, suggesting that intellectual maturity is relevant to their performance. Moreover, two of the items (the right-hand figure shown in Fig. 3.3. and an outline of the human body) are closely related to the material of standard, Western cognitive tests – the Bender-Gestalt test (Clawson, 1962, see Fig. 6.4) and the Draw-a-Man Test (Harris, 1963). Zambian children are superior at copying these items in wire, while English children are superior at copying them with pencil and paper. Thus it appears from this study that the effect on Western culture of that great invention by Gutenberg, the printing process, has been rather more limited than Wober (1966) supposed. It is the specific medium of patterns on paper that proves difficult to interpret and use in non-Western cultures, rather than visual media as a whole.

3 Depth perception in the real world

One category of pictures is well known to be especially difficult to perceive: these are the optical or geometric illusions (see A1, A4). In Fig. 6.2, measuring with a ruler may convince us that lines A and B are equal in fact, but the illusion that A looks longer than B remains compelling. The peculiar significance of these demonstrations is that they are apparently reliable instances of a generally efficient psychological function breaking down. One theory for explaining this phenomenon is that mechanisms which are designed to maintain accurate judgements of size irrespective of distance in the three-dimensional world are accidentally triggered by certain features of these two-dimensional, pictorial displays. Thus in the Ponzo illusion (see Fig. 6.2) the tendency for the upper line to appear longer may arise from the frequency with which converging straight lines like those in the figure occur as a perspective cue to distance in the real world. The eye is thus tricked into scaling up the perceived size of the upper line, as if it were more distant than the lower one and thus projecting a relatively smaller image on the retina (Gregory, 1970). Similar accounts have been developed for the Müller-Lyer (M-L) and Horizontal-Vertical (H-V) illusions (see Fig. 6.2).

If this kind of explanation is valid we may expect that peoples whose normal experience is based on different physical environments will differ in susceptibility to these pictorial illusions. There is good evidence that certain more elaborate illusions are dependent for their effect on experience of a 'carpentered world' in which straight lines and right-angles

94

are often viewed from various vantage-points. Allport and Pettigrew (1957) found that rural Zulu herd boys, who live in dome-shaped houses without any right-angles, are much less likely (when looking with both eyes open) to misinterpret a rotating trapezoidal window as being rectangular, than are urban Zulu schoolboys of the same age in the modern city of Johannesburg. Another geometrical illusion designed by the same ingenious artist, Ames, was used by Stewart (1974) in a study of several groups in Zambia. The Ames Distorted Room (see A1, p. 72) is a very curious shape but, when viewed through a peephole, it projects the same image to the observer's eye as a normal rectangular room. If the assumption of rect-angularity is made, errors of size estimation occur for objects

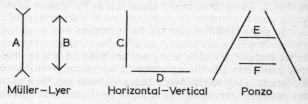

Müller–Lyer   Horizontal–Vertical   Ponzo

Fig. 6.2 *Geometric illusions*

Contrary to appearances, lines A and B are in fact equal in length, as are lines C and D and lines E and F.

placed in various positions in the room, because their relative distance is misjudged. Stewart found that rural Tonga children were less subject to this illusion than children living in the city of Lusaka. She also found a parallel change in susceptibility to the M-L illusion with increasing exposure to a rectangular environment (Stewart, 1973).

Cross-cultural research on the pictorial illusions was first undertaken at the beginning of this century by Rivers (1901), who found an interesting cross-over: non-Westernized people in Papua New Guinea and in India were less susceptible to the M-L illusion than English people, but more susceptible than the English to the H-V illusion. The significance of this pattern was emphasized by Segall, Campbell and Herskovitz (1966), who noted that it could not be dismissed as merely reflecting a general unfamiliarity with pictures. They have proposed that the 'ecological validity' of various cues in these illusion figures may vary independently across different physical environments. The prevalence of right-angles is largely determined by the local mode of technology, whereas foreshortening of lines that fall vertically on the retina (which they see as the origin of the H-V illusion) depends partly on the natural geography of the people's habitat. Thus 'peoples living mostly outdoors in open, spacious environments . . . will be *more* susceptible than Western peoples in urban environments. On the other hand, some non-Western groups should be *less* susceptible to the illusion, e.g. rain forest or canyon dwellers' (Segall *et al.*, 1966:97). The same argument has been advanced for the Ponzo illusion (Brislin, 1974).

Segall and his associates (1966) enlisted the assistance of anthropologists to administer the M-L and H-V illusions in thirteen different communities spread over eight different African countries, and obtained substantial support for their hypotheses. Their data, however, do not fit the theory in every respect, and a number of criticisms have been raised of the study. Jahoda (1966) has stressed the importance of considering the possible effects of exposure to Western education and other cultural variables, which were not analysed in Segall *et al.*'s study. Moreover the theory needs to take account of the fact that susceptibility to the M-L decreases with age. The impact of the environment on the individual's perceptual development must therefore be supposed to occur in the very early years of life. From this it follows:

> that it would be inappropriate to rank subjects' 'carpenteredness' on the basis of their current geographical residence in that it was quite possible that they had spent their early childhood in another locality or had travelled to other localities, where the visual ecologies were different. (Weaver, 1974:21)

To these ecological complexities we must add the fact that the perceptual mechanisms underlying geometrical illusions are still the subject of theoretical controversy, even to the point of questioning whether they are exclusively concerned with vision (Over, 1968). Thus while it has generated some very elegant and precisely formulated studies, the topic of geometric illusions has not yet provided a convincing theoretical framework within which to interpret cultural differences in pictorial perception.

The major thrust of ecological theories of illusion susceptibility is that subjects carry over to pictures their visual inference habits derived from experience of the three-dimensional world. The less a population have developed the skill of judging distance in the real world, the less we may expect them to perceive depth in a pictorial representation. Cole and Scribner

(1974) have presented some provocative 'anecdotal evidence' which to them:

> indicates that there may indeed be cultural (or at least experiential) influences on perception for natural scenes. For example, Turnbull (1961) in his ethnography of the pygmies of the Iturbi forest relates an incident in which a pygmy accompanies him out of the forest. At one point there is an opportunity to see some cows, grazing in the distance. The pygmy, who knows what cows are, but who has never had the opportunity to see one at a great distance, thinks that he is looking at ants! We have observed a similar phenomenon when a jungle-raised Kpelle child is taken at around age 10 to the capital city of Monrovia, where large tanker ships can be seen far at sea from a tall hotel on a hilltop. The child, who had never seen such a view before and was not familiar with tankers, commented on the bravery of men who would go out to sea in such small boats. (1974:97)

The ability to judge the real size of an object irrespective of the distance from which it is observed is known as 'size constancy' (see A4). It depends, of course, on the ability to estimate the distance of the object since the retinal image varies according to distance, although familiarity with the actual size of the object can also help. Size constancy has been studied cross-culturally by Thouless (1932), Beveridge (1935) and Mundy-Castle and Nelson (1962). The first two studies found significantly greater size constancy among Indian students and West African art students than among comparable European adults, while the latter study found significantly lesser size constancy among the isolated Knysna forest workers and among 'black' South African labourers than among Western, educated adults. Since the procedure used in the latter study differed from that of the early studies, it is not clear whether the apparent contradiction arises from procedural or sampling differences. But, in any case, the relevance of these experiments, which involved judgements of size over distances between one and three metres, to Cole and Scribner's (1974) anecdotes is questionable. As Vernon has pointed out, 'at great distances, especially when there is intervening space as in looking down into a valley from the side of a mountain, constancy is greatly reduced' (1970: 147). It is most likely that Cole and Scribner's (1974) observations refer to conditions in which distance cues are insufficient to produce for any observer a *perceptual* experience of size constancy and that under these conditions familiarity leads experienced observers to make an *intellectual* judgement which disregards what is seen in favour of what is known.

It is doubtful whether any human community could survive, however densely forested their environment, without a highly developed capacity to perceive and estimate distance in the real world. Moreover, there is ample evidence to show that this capacity is part of man's biological heritage shared with a wide range of mammals and, if not actually innate, is present to a remarkable degree before children are old enough to explore their environment outside the immediate home (Gibson and Walk, 1960). It is true that the finer judgements of distance continue to develop throughout childhood (Vernon, 1970: 150–1) but the scale of these improvements is far too small to suggest a learned basis for depth perception which might account for all the cross-cultural differences in response to pictorial materials. The search for an explanation along these lines is probably a result of the biasing effect of a Western cultural upbringing. As Herskovitz (1959) observed, 'to those of us accustomed to the idiom of the realism of the photographic lens, the degree of conventionalisation that inheres in even the clearest, most accurate photograph, is something of a shock' (1959:56). It is to the details of these conventions that we now turn.

4 Detection, recognition and identification of pictures

Anthropological and other informal reports by Europeans coming into contact with peoples unfamiliar with Western culture have from time to time described reactions indicating a total failure to detect anything of significance on a picture or photograph (Deregowski, Muldrow and Muldrow 1972). According to Muldrow's initial observation, adult members of the Me'en tribe, who live in a region of Ethiopia which is still very remote from any Western cultural influence, responded to drawings of animals by feeling, smelling, tasting and rustling the paper without showing any interest in the visual appearance of the picture itself. The suspicion that these unorthodox reactions were due to the unfamiliarity of paper was confirmed in the follow-up study, which used drawings painted on cloth, a substance with which these people were familiar. In this case without exception they 'did not get distracted by the nature of the material and responded to the pictures shown' (1972:422). Another difference between the original stimuli and those which communicated better was the size of the figures. On the cloth, the animals which were generally recognized were about 30 cm high as compared with a height of less than 5 cm in the original of Fig. 6.1.

Miller offers the following speculation:

> It is possible to see that a picture represents some object without recognizing just exactly what that object is. The first perception [which Dember, 1960 would classify as *detection*] ... is to some degree an all-or-none phenomenon. If an individual has never learned that a picture may represent some object, he will not be able to perceive any object when first presented with a picture. (1973:13–18)

Considering the results of the Me'en study this may be too strong a statement. The authors state that their Lowland sample of girls are extremely unlikely to have ever seen a picture before. In spite of this, seven out of ten correctly identified the first cloth picture as a buck and all correctly identified the second as a leopard. Given a sufficiently salient stimulus, with distracting cues removed such as the novelty of paper or the distinct white band of the border, immediate recognition may be possible simply by stimulus generalization, one of the most basic characteristics of learning (see A3).

Nevertheless an intermediary condition may exist where 'if an individual has only one set of cues at his disposal (i.e. those that lead him to expect to see an object in a picture), he will not recognize the object depicted even though he is able to perceive that *some* object is depicted' (Miller, 1973:138). Thus several of the Lowland Me'en subjects misidentified the buck and the leopard as other four-legged animals, and in several cases recognition seems to have been built up gradually by an accumulation of information as the experimenter guided the subject's attention to the various details by tracing the outline of the animal with a finger. The authors note the similarity in this respect of their subjects' verbal responses to those of young American children in a task which presented successively clearer and clearer images for identification starting with a completely blurred image (Potter, 1966).

Another way of simplifying the task of interpreting a picture is to limit the number of alternatives which it might be taken to represent. In this situation we can inquire whether the subject is able to recognize an object when it is represented pictorially without requiring him to identify it by name. Thus Deregowski (1968b) gave a recognition task to boys and men in a 'relatively pictureless' Bisa community living in a region of Zambia remote from the main arterial roads. The task was to pick out from an array of eighteen model animals the model represented in a black and white photograph. Six of the animals were commonly to be seen in the area, while the others were very exotic. The boys, who had had more school education, were better at finding the strange animals than the men, while the adults, who were mainly hunters, performed better with the pictures of familiar animals. The main finding of theoretical interest, however, is that in nine of the twenty-five cases where a man was unable to identify either the picture or the model as any creature he knew, he was still able to recognize which model the photograph represented.

In conclusion we can see that pictures are by no means automatically successful devices for communication. But efforts to eliminate distracting features do improve their effectiveness, and under optimal conditions they seem to be recognizable without any prior learning. Moreover people with very little experience of pictures can sometimes recognize photographs of totally unfamiliar objects. I stress these points because they reinforce the view that most pictures are not entirely arbitrary representations of the real world. Whereas it is impossible to guess what most words represent unless we have learned the language, the relation between pictures and their referents is one of similarity, albeit of varying degrees. The arbitrariness of pictures lies in what features they choose to stress and what features to leave out, and it is the conventions governing this choice which the experienced picture perceiver must learn.

5 Pictorial cues to the third dimension

Hudson (1960) and Deregowski (1968a) found that the ability to identify the various items in Fig. 6.1 was no guarantee that a subject would interpret three-dimensionally the spatial relations among them. This need not surprise us when we realize that the cues required to identify the elephant and the hill can hardly include their size, since both are evidently much smaller than the objects they represent. One of the main cues in this picture to the relative distance among the man, the elephant and the antelope is their relative size against the background knowledge of the normal sizes of these creatures. Knowing that the elephant is a much larger animal than the others, we can infer that, since its image is smaller than theirs, it must represent a distant elephant (from us and hence from the man). The experienced picture perceiver, however, does not reach this conclusion by a process of reasoning: he perceives the spatial relationship automatically because he has learned that Western artists use the cue of relative size to represent distance.

Other cues which Hudson (1960) included in his original series of drawings are overlap and perspective. Thus we can see in Fig. 6.1 that the image of the antelope overlaps that of the first hill which in turn overlaps that of the second hill on which the elephant is standing. In another drawing of the series, the elephant and tree were depicted near the apex of a pair of converging straight lines representing a road. The convergence of lines which can be assumed to be parallel constitutes the well-known cue to recession, which we saw in section 3 of this chapter may be responsible for the Ponzo illusion (see Fig. 6.2). Since the laws of perspective were a late discovery in European art (see Gombrich, 1960) and the assumption of parallel edges to a road is promoted by a 'carpentered' environment, it is not too surprising to learn that African children seldom understand this cue. The cue of overlap which, if it is noticed, can hardly be misinterpreted, was found by Hudson (1960) to be the most effective of his three cues and Kilbride, Robbins and Freeman (1968) confirmed this result with a cross-section of Ugandan schoolchildren.

In order to understand why so few of these schoolchildren in South Africa, Uganda, Ghana (Mundy-Castle, 1966) and Zambia (Deregowski, 1968a) show an appreciation of depth in Hudson's pictures, we need to contrast the 3-D cues we have listed above with the cues indicating flatness in the same pictures. One of the most powerful cues to depth perception in the real world arise from the fact that we have two eyes which receive different images of the same object (*binocular disparity*). Another is that, as we move around, the images projected by objects at different distances from us change their relative positions on the retina (*motion parallax*) (see A4). Both of these cues indicate to the brain that pictures are flat objects with no depth. The difference in image at the two eyes is the same for the elephant and the antelope in Fig. 6.1, whereas if the elephant were really farther away from us binocular disparity of its image would be less than for the antelope. When we move our head to the right there is no tendency in Fig. 6.1 for the image of the antelope to become superimposed on that of the elephant: yet this is just what would happen if we were looking at the real world scene which the figure depicts. Thus

101

two of the most powerful cues for depth perception in the real world contradict the pictorial depth cues. This is not an isolated feature of this particular illustration: it is a universal characteristic of drawings and photographs. It is only the Western convention that teaches us to suspend the information which indicates flatness and focus our attention on the much weaker pictorial depth cues.

Binocular disparity can be simulated in pictures by the use of stereoscopic techniques (see Gregory, 1970 for a vivid range of illustrations). The basic principle is to present separately to the two eyes the two different images which an object

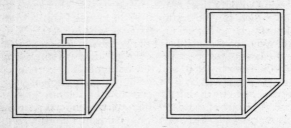

Fig. 6.3 *Diagrams used in Deregowski's construction task*

Deregowski (1968 a) found that more Zambian children built 3-D models of these figures than interpreted Fig. 6.1 in 3-D, but even on this test many subjects responded in 2-D.

or scene would project in the real world. This can be done either by lodging two different pictures behind the lenses of a pair of binoculars, or by asking the observer to wear different coloured lenses over the two eyes and superimposing the two images appropriately displaced in the same two colours (each lens then filters out one image so that only the other image reaches that eye). Using the latter technique Deregowski (1974) showed that a majority of Kenyan schoolboys who interpreted the diagram on the right in Fig. 6.3 as a two-dimensional pattern, saw similar figures in depth when presented stereoscopically. The fact that some did not shows that even binocular disparity is not always sufficient to induce 3-D perception of pictures.

Among the pictorial depth cues one of the most powerful was omitted from Hudson's (1960) pictures. This is what Gibson (1950) has called the *gradient of density*. Two examples are shown in Fig. 6.4. In each case the individual components of the pattern get smaller and closer together as the surface they represent recedes: the overall texture of the surface has a density which gradually increases with distance. Wohlwill (1965) found that these gradients are more important as depth cues in pictures than in three-dimensional displays for Western subjects over a wide range of ages. Kingsley, Allison and Noble (unpublished) commissioned an artist to redraw one of Hudson's perspective drawings with the addition of pebbles on the road and grass in the open terrain, each surface showing a gradient of density, while all other features remained the same. A class of Grade 6 urban Zambian children gave 64 per cent of 3-D responses to this version as compared with only 53 per cent in a similar class presented with the plain line drawing. A third class who saw a coloured version complete with density gradients and haze around the distant items gave 76 per cent of 3-D responses. It is probably significant that the only photograph in Hudson's (1960) test series was entirely devoid of density gradients.

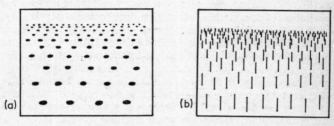

Fig. 6.4 *Examples of density gradients, a pictorial cue to depth*
Example A might be pebbles on the ground. Example B might be a stretch of grass.

We have seen now that there is a wide variety of cues to distance which the human eye can use. Some of these can never be included in a picture and indeed tell the eye that a picture is flat. This is why pictures can never really trick the eye completely. But a large category of cues can be included in highly realistic representations (notably photographs) and the evidence reviewed above suggests that the more of these the artist includes, the greater the likelihood that unsophisticated observers will see depth in his picture. We should note, however, that the attempt to create this kind of illusion is itself an artistic convention which is by no means shared by all styles (Gombrich, 1960). We shall return to the implications of that fact in section (8) of this chapter. Meanwhile it must be clear that we cannot interpret comparisons between 3-D perception scores obtained by different populations when they have been tested with different materials (e.g. Dawson, Young and Choi, 1974).

6 *Orientation of abstract shapes*

Another feature of Western pictures which has proved confusing to many unsophisticated observers is the orientation of abstract shapes. A number of tests, such as Koh's Block Design Test shown in Fig. 3.1, require the subject to copy an abstract design either by drawing or by assembling components like blocks or tiles. Several studies using these tests in Africa noted that the reproduced design was often tilted unconventionally on the table or paper relative to the standard (Maistriaux, 1955; McFie, 1961). One interpretation which could be offered for these observations is that orientation, like pictorial depth cues, is not a salient feature of the stimulus array unless one has been taught to pay attention to it. Indeed Gibson, Gibson, Pick and Osser (1962) advanced just such a hypothesis to account for the increase in sensitivity to orientation in a matching task by American children in the first few years of school. The difficulty experienced by many young children in telling apart the letters b, d, p and q (Davidson, 1935) leads to a special emphasis on discrimination of orientation when learning to read.

Not all differences in orientation, however, are difficult for young children to distinguish. Rudel and Teuber (1963) found that the pairs A and C in Fig. 6.5 were much easier to tell apart than B and D for pre-school American children. Exactly the same order of difficulty is experienced by young Zambian children, whether they live in the city or a remote rural area (Serpell, 1971a). Part of this has to do with how the figures are displayed relative to one another, and whether the child has to remember one of a pair over several trials or merely to detect the difference (Bryant, 1974). But it does seem likely that the discriminability of one orientation from another is partly a consequence of how the human brain is designed (Corballis and Beale, 1970).

Shapiro (1960) noticed that the tilted reproductions of Koh's designs were not entirely random. Further analysis has shown that they tend to move towards greater symmetry and stability (Deregowski, 1972). Indeed the paradox is that far from ignoring orientation, unsophisticated subjects seem to follow very definite preferences for certain orientations of abstract geometrical shapes (Braine, 1973). The features which decide which way up a figure 'looks best' are fairly complex, but they seem to be much the same for Zambian and American children (Ghent, 1961; Serpell, 1971b). This finding should alert us to the danger of overextending the carpentered-world hypothesis: although geometrical shapes are less extensively used in African cultures than in the West, the perceptual laws which govern

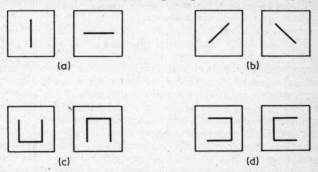

Fig. 6.5 *Pairs of geometrical shapes for discrimination of orientation*

Pairs A and C are discriminated more easily than pairs B and D.

how they are seen should not be *assumed* to be irrelevant outside Western culture. Some of them may arise from structural features of the human brain and body quite independently of cultural conditioning (Appelle, 1972).

Orientation is, of course, the basic feature to be adjusted in Witkin's rod-and-frame test (see Ch. 3, p. 40), and some authors have tried to link the tendency to rotate a figure when copying it to field-dependency (Blum and Chagnon, 1967). But we must be wary of extrapolating from one culture to another in the explanations we offer for this phenomenon (see Fig. 3.4). In Western clinical practice, rotation of Koh's designs is widely regarded as an index of brain damage (Yates, 1956). In African populations such rotations are quite normal. It seems that the cultural difference lies in whether the (universally) preferred orientation is allowed to dominate the response. The convention of aligning a drawing with the edge of the paper is clearly instilled by education. In African schools where drawing receives little emphasis the convention is apparently less well taught. This may in fact increase the difficulty of copying tasks since following a set procedure can simplify the processing of information (see A4). In trying to copy a complex figure subjects often tilt their head and turn the paper around to get a different view. By the end of a series of such adjustments it must be easy to lose track if one is not matching the orientation to a definite frame of reference. Thus Jahoda (in press) has shown that Ghanaian schoolboys align the orientation least well for figures they have spent a long time copying.

7 *Pictorial education*

Several writers have been sufficiently impressed by the difficulties experienced by African schoolchildren with pictorial perception to undertake training programmes to see how best the necessary skills can be taught. A very limited attempt with three classes of Grade 7 urban Zambian children resulted in only marginal improvement (Serpell and Deregowski, 1972). Only four class periods spread over two weeks were spent explaining the conventions and illustrating them either with the use of photographs and diagrams or with films. Two weeks later pictorial depth perception tests showed that most children had not changed, although among those who did change there was a reliable positive trend. Dawson (1967) gave a much more intensive course of eight weekly sessions to a group of twelve mine apprentices in Sierra Leone. These pupils were required to trace the outlines of scenery on a window and then to sketch their window drawings on to paper, as well as drawing directly on paper. Three months later they showed a significant improvement on the tests from a mean score of 6 per cent to 43 per cent 3-D responses.

It seems probable that a major factor in the success of Dawson's class was the inclusion of first-hand experience in the activity of drawing. Held (1965) and others have emphasized the special opportunities for perceptual reorganization which are afforded by perceptual motor activity. Duncan, Gourlay and Hudson describe a 'portable view window' which can be used for the tracing procedure and report that it has been used successfully with Congolese adults (1973:168). We should beware, however, of assuming that drawing ability is a necessary precondition for understanding drawings. Few people in the West, for instance, are capable of drawing a

106

human figure in correct proportions or a landscape in accordance with the laws of perspective. But without the training required for the mastery of these production techniques, most Western observers are still highly sensitive to distortions in other people's drawings. Indeed the principle that receptive control precedes expressive control is very widespread in human development. Many more people can tell when a singer is out of tune or off the beat than can sing in tune and keep time in their own amateur performance. And in language Berko and Brown (1960:528) describe how a young child will often reject in an adult's speech the very mistake in articulation which he himself seems unable to avoid.

Perhaps the important distinction to be made between learning to draw and learning to interpret pictures lies in the complexity of the response. We know that much more is involved in drawing than the perception of significant cues (Freeman, 1972; Goodnow and Levine, 1973) and it seems extravagant to insist on teaching all those additional skills merely for the sake of ensuring comprehension of other people's drawings and photographs. Moreover the issue of indoctrination looms much larger once we begin to teach children how to draw (see section 8). Perceptual adaptation can be effected without motor activity if the appropriate information is provided (Howard and Templeton, 1966). Perceptual learning theories would suggest that the distinctive features of pictorial depth cues could be taught by making quite simple responses contingent on discriminating just those cues. This would require not so much inducing depth perception by supplementing the existing cues (Deregowski, 1974) but rather emphasizing those cues which are normally present in pictures but do not control the subjects' perception or attention.

The idea of teaching children to understand pictures is relatively new. A much better established tradition exists which stresses the usefulness of pictures as teaching aids (Ball and Byrnes, 1960; Bowman, 1968). This school of thought has permeated modern Western education, so that teachers in training are bombarded with catch-phrases like 'A picture is worth a thousand words'. Increasingly modern textbooks are heavily illustrated with diagrams, drawings and photographs. There can be little doubt from the evidence we have reviewed that much of this visual enrichment programme in education goes unheeded in countries outside the industrialized countries of the West. Children in the Zambian classes whom we attempted to teach (Serpell and Deregowski, 1972) often did not understand the illustrations in their textbooks, and other reports suggest that even some trained science teachers have difficulty interpreting many of the standard diagrams relating to scientific concepts they are required to teach.

8 *The question of artistic style*

Much of the discussion in previous sections of this chapter has implied that the Western style of pictorial art represents the real world in an objectively correct fashion. By implication the individual who does not understand this convention is making a mistake. Yet, as Gombrich has pointed out, 'the first prejudice teachers of art appreciation usually try to combat is the belief that artistic excellence is identical with photographic accuracy' (1960:4). Is it not possible then that subjects in different cultures 'reject' Western art forms and photographs on aesthetic grounds, and that all the literature described above has mistakenly described a stylistic preference as a difficulty in perception?

A small number of studies have directly asked non-Western subjects which of a variety of representations they prefer. Hudson (1962) and Deregowski (1969b, 1970) found that African subjects with limited Western education slightly preferred unfolded, 'split', 'developed' or 'chain-type' drawings like Fig. 6.6*a* or *b* to orthogonal representations like *c* and *d*. The reasons for such a preference often refer to the fact that the perspective picture fails to show some of the important features. There have even been reports of African subjects interpreting a foreshortened representation of a human limb as representing an amputation (Hudson, 1967). But Duncan, Gourlay and Hudson (1973) found that such misinterpretations were extremely rare among even their youngest, Standard 1, rural Zulu children in South Africa.

The discussion of why such styles prevail in, for instance, North and South American indigenous art leads rapidly into the realm of speculation (Lévi-Strauss, 1963). One mistake we should certainly avoid is that of equating the origins of such art forms with those of 'primitive' attempts by young children to represent the world as they know it (Werner, 1940). Few art historians would accept that the famous painters of fourteenth-century Italy had childish or under-developed minds; yet their renderings of scenes and objects also share certain features with those of young Western children's art (Gombrich, 1960).

One of the key problems here is the meaning of 'realism' in art. The development of the camera lens with its one-to-one correspondence between the outside world and the film has led to a widespread misconception that photographs can capture what the human eye really sees. But a stationary, single retinal image is no more what we see than the pattern of nerve cells which fire on the wrinkled surface of the visual cortex in our brain (see A2). It is merely that this particular step in the complex transformation of physical energy into mental experi-

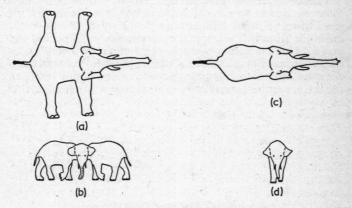

Fig. 6.6 *Various ways of drawing an elephant*

ence has received a great deal of attention in the development of Western science. Realistic or, as Gombrich calls it, 'illusionist' art is a matter of 'inventing comparisons which work' (1960: 254). The artist 'enriches our experience because he offers us an equivalence within his medium that may also "work" for us' (1960:276).

For most functional purposes a very abstract representation which specifies certain distinctive features is sufficient to ensure communication between artist and observer. Thus considerations of symmetry and other aesthetic features of form can determine within very wide limits the artist's mode of representation without loss of communicative efficiency. The more symbolic such abstract art becomes the more it relies on a fund of common experience with the art form itself shared by the artist and his audience. Thus Duncan *et al.* (1973) found that the small lines used by Western cartoonists to imply

motion were the least understood of all the pictorial conventions
they presented to rural African schoolchildren. And where the
artist had drawn the head of a boy in three different positions
above the same trunk to indicate that he was turning his head
around, about half the children concluded that the boy represented was deformed. Likewise Western observers require the
guidance of an anthropologist to understand the art forms of
American Indians (Boas, 1927) or Nuba personal art in the
Sudan (Faris, 1972).

Gombrich (1960) has documented very thoroughly how
Western art has been constrained in its development by the
need to retain a link with cultural tradition. But he does not
conclude from this that stylistic conventions are arbitrary and
static. 'There is such a thing as a real visual discovery', such
that the impressionist school of painters in the nineteenth century 'taught' the public 'not, indeed, to see nature with an
innocent eye, but to explore an unexpected alternative that

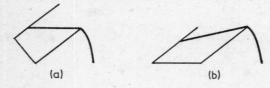

(a)   (b)

Fig. 6.7 *Scientific diagrams*

A secondary school science teacher in Zambia reports that
Form V 'pupils asked to *copy* from the blackboard the diagram
on the left, showing water being poured from a beaker, produced,
in an alarming number of cases, the diagram shown on the right'
(Bingham, 1968:2).

turned out to fit certain experiences better than did any earlier
paintings' (1960:275). It seems possible that this is also the
nature of certain modern Western conventions regarding perspective and orientation. These have been linked quite closely
to the development of physical science and it may well be that
their emphasis on the static view from a given position (the
'here and now') is an essential aid to understanding some scientific concepts. For instance, the child who redraws Fig. 6.7a as
Fig. 6.7b, perhaps for reasons of aesthetic preference, is likely
to become confused about the nature of horizontality. The
drawing b might be as good as a for representing a glass of
water, but only a enables the observer to predict the event

of the water spilling as the glass is tipped. Thus the skills of pictorial perception in the Western mode may constitute an irreplacable 'amplifying tool' (Cole and Bruner, 1971) for the application of the child's cognitive processes in learning about modern science and technology.

If the teaching of modern science requires us to contemplate instructing schoolchildren in certain modes of representation, this need not necessarily mean that their aesthetic self-expression must be forced within the Western style. The problem is perhaps less critical in sub-Saharan Africa where the traditional modes of visual art have only seldom attempted to represent the spatial relations of the real world on flat surfaces. But we know as yet very little about the interaction in the individual between mutually incompatible picture styles. It may be difficult, if not impossible, to introduce a Chinese or Indian student to Western scientific diagrams without the new modes of perception and interpretation infiltrating his aesthetic outlook in ways incompatible with the traditions of Eastern art. If so, the dilemma faced by educators reflects that same point of conflict we considered in Chapter 4, where the impact of Western culture threatens to undermine a cherished value in a different cultural system.

7
Theories, methods and applications

In this concluding chapter, we will consider in reverse order the objectives outlined in Chapter 1. First I shall ask what we have learned from cross-cultural psychology about the generality of psychological theories, and suggest some reasons for the rather poor returns on that score from research so far. Then we will briefly review the findings on the psychological problems of adaptation faced by people in situations of rapid social change. Finally I shall suggest some implications of the research we have reviewed for the range of applications open to psychology in developing countries.

Psychological theory and method in cross-cultural studies

The great majority of cross-cultural studies have tackled the question of how general are theories developed in the West by direct confrontation. They set out to replicate a procedure developed in the West with a different cultural sample and enquire whether the same or similar results obtain. If the theory is that of Witkin (see Ch. 3), the questions are (1) does performance on EFT correlate with that on RFT? (2) do males obtain more field-independent scores than females? and finally (3) can we relate cross-cultural differences on these tests to the features of child-rearing which Witkin's theory has proposed as antecedents of individual differences and sex differences in the West? If the theory is that of Piaget (see Ch. 5), the analogous questions posed are (1) do children in different cultures make the same kind of logical error in conservation or classification tasks? (2) does performance on the tasks follow the same developmental sequence and at the same ages as in the West? and finally (3) can we interpret in terms of Piaget's theory those cross-cultural differences in test performance which occur?

Interpretation of the answers to these questions is, as we have seen, controversial. But are these the most profitable questions for cross-cultural research to ask? If the answers were all positive, then the results would indeed serve to extend the generality of our understanding of those areas of human behaviour. But where the answers have been negative, theoretical explanations of what has gone wrong tend to focus on limited aspects of the test procedure. Perhaps EFT is phrased in an unfamiliar medium for Africans with little experience of Western education. Perhaps the test for conservation of quantity mystifies children who are not used to watching a formal demonstration by a person of authority. These detailed criticisms of Western test procedures suggest the need for caution in our interpretation of cross-cultural differences. But they do not generate any radical new theoretical insights into the nature of behaviour either in the culture under study or on a universal plane.

One recurrent feature of the studies reviewed in earlier chapters is that performance on experimental tasks (whether of motivation or cognition) typically shows either no cross-cultural difference or Western superiority. This pattern used once to be interpreted as evidence of Western man's 'advancement' or 'superiority'. More recently researchers have become aware that it arises from the 'centri-cultural' strategy of research outlined above, in which we ask 'how well can *they* do *our* tricks?' (Wober, 1969). A few studies have set out to illustrate this fact by selecting instances of tasks which are similar in general structure (category sorting; copying forms) to one on which Western subjects do well, but which are less familiar to Westerners than to another group. When this is done the non-Western group performs better on the task whose elements are familiar to them, and the Western group performs better on the Western version of the task (Irwin, Schafer and Feiden, 1974; Serpell, 1974). The same 'cross-over' design is present for some of the groups in Segall, Campbell and Herskovitz' (1966) study of visual illusions (see Ch. 6).

Evidence of this kind is consonant with Cole *et al.*'s conclusion that 'cultural differences . . . reside more in the situations to which particular . . . processes are applied than in the

113

existence of a process in one cultural group and its absence in another' (1971:233) – which was cited in relation to their studies of cognition in Chapter 5. Thus what is needed, as Bartlett pointed out many years ago, is 'knowledge about the social determination of the significance of simple stimuli and situations' (1937:414). Performance on any task is jointly determined by several factors. Not only is there the well-known complementary relation between motivation and cognition (discussed at the beginning of Ch. 3). There is also a range of cognitive and perceptual skills combining in performance, some of which have been overlooked by studies confined to a population in which certain skills are universally present. Thus cross-cultural psychology can claim a major responsibility for drawing attention to the perceptual skills required for understanding pictures (Ch. 6). It took comparison with a group in whom the skills were lacking to bring them into focus as a separate aspect of behaviour, at least partially independent of visual perception of the solid world.

If such task-specific skills are the rule rather than the exception, we should expect to find a number of them in every cultural group which are tied to the distinctive artefacts and activities of that group. Anthropologists have often drawn attention to the high level of skill displayed in the art forms of different communities, such as the playing of musical instruments. Yet psychological research has scarcely ever taken these skills as the starting-point for cross-cultural investigation. Similarly Hopkins and Wober (1973) have pointed out how little systematic research has looked at games and sports across cultures, although their conventionalization makes them obvious candidates for analysis as vehicles of cultural tradition. One reason for this was noted by Berrien:

> With the emphasis on developing countries, investigators are fanning out from those countries where research techniques have reached a higher level of sophistication into those where the supply of indigenous skilled researchers is severely restricted. These emissaries necessarily carry with them their ethnic biases which shape the significance and the definition of problems. Because of their great scientific armamentation and sophisticated technical methodology developed in, and appropriate to their home environments, there may be a tendency to overwhelm the host researchers into accepting totally inappropriate research issues and methodologies. (1967:38)

Now it will reasonably be objected by some of these researchers that their choice of topic is dictated not by intuitive speculation, but by a careful assessment of scientifically established theory. But we have only to look at the variety of conflicting theories that have gained support within the Western academic world, to realize that other factors beyond 'science' contribute to the acceptance of theory. The intellectual traditions which led Piaget and the Kendlers (see Ch. 5) to propose their very different interpretations of children's cognitive development are no less intimately tied up with Western culture than the less respectable ethnic biases which find expression in Western myths of racial superiority (see F8).

A number of writers have noted the similarity between this problem faced by cross-cultural researchers in various disciplines and the task of describing a new language. The phonemes of one language (as we saw in Ch. 4) simply will not do as descriptive categories for the sound system of another language. The system of *phonetics*, which is supposed to represent the sounds of all languages in an objective way, acts as a bridge in this task between the *phonemic* description of one language and another. Only linguists become familiar with the 'outsider's view' of language sounds called phonetics; whereas the natural speakers of each language have at least an implicit knowledge of the 'insider's' phonemic description best suited to that language. The physical sciences aspire to give an objective or outsider's view of what they describe; but the social sciences are not so clear on this point. Many anthropologists, for instance, feel that their task is – like that of identifying the phonemes of a language – to provide an insider's view of the culture they are studying. Yet some of the standard concepts of social science are used as if they represent objective, outsider's view categories like the linguist's phonetic symbols.

> Such terms as 'religion', 'property', or 'schizophrenia' are only dubiously to be ascribed to the frame of reference for the outside view, and until a particular community has been studied one cannot know if they are relevant for the inside view of that community. Hence, a proposal to investigate the religion of some largely unstudied community constitutes a projection from one inside view – that of Western culture – into another. Such cross-cultural projections are inevitable as an ethnographer begins his work; the work is not complete until they have been eliminated. (Hockett, 1964:126)

We noted in Chapter 2 that some mental patients in Africa present symptoms characteristic of schizophrenia except for one notable difference (the prospect of recovery). Should we then revise our concept of schizophrenia, saying that it has better prospects of recovery in some cultures than in others? Or should we conclude that this concept, which has proved useful in describing Western patients, is simply not applicable to the description of African mental illness?

Berry (1969) suggests that we can overcome this problem by a three-stage procedure. First, we project an insider's concept from our own culture A on to another culture B. Second, we modify the concept until it fits in the new culture as a description of behaviour which is 'functionally equivalent' to what the original concept described in culture A. Finally, we take just those elements shared by these two insider's-view concepts to define a 'derived' outsider's-view concept applicable to both A and B. If this procedure is followed for a large number of different cultures we should end up with a 'universal' concept similar to the linguist's phonetic categories. As Berrien (1967) points out, it is our present lack of such universal categories which constitutes the main impediment to arriving at a detached and objective or, as he puts it, 'Olympian view of cross-cultural data' (p. 44).

The most difficult step in the procedure outlined by Berry (1969) is that of identifying 'functionally equivalent' realms of behaviour across two or more cultures. For, as Campbell (1964) argues, this is a task like that of matching two pictures: if we focus our attention on the smallest elements, it is almost impossible to say which part of one newspaper photograph corresponds to a given item in another copy of the photograph. We need the overall pattern or gestalt to guide us. Likewise it is easier to be sure that one has translated accurately between two languages when dealing with a whole paragraph than with a single word. So in cross-cultural comparisons 'it takes acquaintance with the larger cultural context to identify the appropriate parallel or classificatory assignment of any particular item' (1964:330–1). This broader perspective, as we saw in Chapter 2, is a defining characteristic of the anthropological approach. Hence both Campbell and Berry, like Cole and his associates (1971), have stressed the relevance of that discipline to research in cross-cultural psychology.

Unfortunately, however, the 'descriptive, humanistic' style of most anthropology is difficult to reconcile with the 'abstractive, hypothesis testing' approach of experimental psychology. Moreover the likelihood of subjective distortion is most marked when dealing with such abstract and indirectly inferred aspects

116

of a culture as its overall pattern or ethos (Campbell, 1961). The problem facing the psychologist is 'to discover techniques which will allow the transition from the analysis of a cultural system to that of regularities in behaviour relating to this system' (Tajfel, 1969:358). In so doing it is very appropriate that he should look to the other social sciences and even to creative literature for hypotheses about what makes the culture tick. But it is probably unrealistic to hope that he will find in such accounts any more objective a structure than those projected from Western psychological theories. Perhaps the most we can hope for is to invent, as Gombrich (1960) put it for illusionist art (see Ch. 6), 'comparisons which work'. And here, of course, much depends on our audience, since, as Berrien (1967) notes, their cultural experience will define the 'anchor point' with reference to which they evaluate any interpretation we propose.

In summary, it seems that cross-cultural psychology has suffered from conservatism in the use of theory. This has arisen partly from ethnocentric bias, researchers being more interested in whether features of their own culture exist elsewhere. Another aggravating constraint has been the preference, perhaps for convenience, for working with established tests. Even selection among the available Western tests has often been dictated by the limitations of the foreign psychologist's competence – hence the predominance of studies by largely non-verbal methods. But above all most researchers have been prevented from considering radical alternatives by their inability to see the behaviour they are studying both within its cultural context and from an insider's perspective. As more psychologists enter the field from varying, non-Western cultural backgrounds we may hope to see an increase in such approaches. The first target of their study in my view should be the experimental analysis of features of behaviour which are distinctive to their culture. From there quite new theoretical generalizations may emerge which will increase our awareness that both emotionally and intellectually 'there is more than one way to skin a cat' (Greenfield, 1966:256).

Economic development and applications of psychology

The analysis I have given above of how psychological theories might come to be seen as valid in different cultures is generally consistent with the position of *cultural relativism* espoused by

Berry (1973) and by Cole and Bruner (1971). What is valid in one culture may not be valid for another. But as we saw in Chapter 1, most politicians in the modern world speak as if economic development is a universally desirable change in man's environment. This has led some psychologists and sociologists to conclude that those values, attitudes and skills which are positively related to economic productivity in technologically advanced countries need to be actively fostered in countries where they are lacking, as part of the drive towards economic development. My own contention is that each of these components of behaviour needs to be examined afresh in the particular cultural context of a given developing country, before we jump to such a conclusion.

I suggested in Chapter 4 that it is wrong to suppose that only through one of the languages of technologically advanced nations can a developing country promote in its children the necessary intellectual skills for participation in a modern economy. If the reasons for choosing a given language as the medium of education are allowed by the policy-makers to go beyond considerations of immediate financial cost, the criteria which deserve priority are complex and controversial. While various psychological factors may have a place in the list, the evidence does not support the view that any language is intrinsically incapable of acting as a medium of abstract, scientific or modern thought. Likewise the evidence (Ch. 2) that belief in the power of witchcraft can coexist in the same person with an understanding of Western science should make us wary of assuming that a total restructuring of attitudes and values is required before a society can make the transition into the world of modern technology. The phenomenon of code-switching (Ch. 4) illustrates the ability of a single human being to use culturally diverse forms of behaviour each in its appropriate context.

On the other hand some of the 'amplifying tools' (Cole and Bruner, 1971) developed by Western culture may be inextricably linked to facets of modern technology which are widely sought after in the rest of the world. If labour-saving machinery, preventive medicine and long-distance communication facilities are to play a part in any country's economic development, some of its citizens at least will need to acquire a number of specialized skills. Scientific and technical training as practised in the West tends to presuppose that certain preliminary skills, including those of pictorial perception, have been developed at an earlier stage. The research reviewed in Chapter 6 suggests that in some societies more explicit instruction is needed in this

118

field at school than has normally been offered in the West.

Some writers have suggested that this kind of 'remedial intervention' in the education of children from non-Western home environments needs to be aimed at fostering more general aspects of Western behaviour. Thus McClelland favours social intervention to promote 'achievement motivation' (Ch. 2), Witkin to promote 'field-independence' (Ch. 3), de Lemos to promote Piaget's sequence of 'conceptual development' (Ch. 5), and Vernon (1969) to promote 'intelligence'. I have argued in the chapters cited that the tests which have been used in cross-cultural research to measure these various qualities of mind are biased in their form so as to favour Western subjects. Thus the evidence is inconclusive as to whether different cultural environments promote these qualities to the same degree as a middle-class Western upbringing. It would, of course, be absurd to institute special educational programmes merely to enable children to perform well on Western tests, if the underlying qualities, which the tests are designed to measure, are in fact already promoted by their normal environment.

Unfortunately this absurdity is well known to occur quite regularly in competitive systems of education: it is known as drilling or 'cramming' for exams. In Zambia, where selection of one in five primary school leavers for places in secondary school is based not only on examinations but partly on a Western type of 'intelligence test', children are carefully prepared by their teachers in the skills of taking IQ tests. No doubt individual differences continue to contribute to differences in performance on the tests in spite of this preparation. But whether these are individual differences in intelligence (defined, for instance, by Wechsler, 1944, as 'the global capacity of the individual to act purposefully, to think rationally, and to deal effectively with his environment') is far from clear. It seems likely that at least an equally important contribution to scores on the tests in this population comes from individual differences in familiarity with the specific conventions of Western cultural adaptation to the environment.

The design and administration of mental tests, used to select individuals for further education or for responsible jobs in industry (see E2), is at the present time the most highly developed application of psychology in countries of the third world (Cronbach and Drenth, 1974). In view of the grave doubts attached to the validity of most of these tests, we may pause to consider whether the efforts of educational and industrial psychologists might not be better directed to other ends.

Rather than trying to select those who (by whatever combination of natural ability and disposition with privileged opportunity) have already learned to deal with the modern environment, a more valuable exercise might be to devise ways of reducing the friction between the majority and that environment. On the one hand there is great scope for improving the efficiency of teaching methods in schools and training methods in industry. On the other hand a still more challenging task is presented by the need to adapt those borrowed Western institutions, the factory and the school, to conform better with the aspirations and skills of other cultural groups.

Appendix
Statistical correlation

The term correlation is based on a statistical computation. In general when two measures are positively correlated across individuals, this means that an individual who scores highly on one test tends to score highly on the other test while low scores on one test are associated with low scores on the other. A negative correlation is when high scores on one test are associated with low scores on the other.

There are several statistical measures of correlation. The most commonly used in psychology is the product-moment correlation coefficient 'r' which can range from -1.00 (for a perfect negative correlation) to $+1.00$ (for a perfect positive correlation). A value of r close to 0.00 indicates that two measures are essentially unrelated or independent of one another.

One of the advantages of computing this statistic is that we can estimate from its mathematical properties how likely it is that the degree of association found between our two measures is due to pure chance. When a correlation is said to be statistically significant, or reliable, this means that the probability that it could have occurred by chance in actually unrelated sets of observations (numbers drawn from two hats, for example) is very low (by convention in psychology, usually less than 5 times in 100). When a correlation is non-significant by this criterion, this is normally interpreted as meaning that we can have very little confidence that the apparent relationship between the two measures is a real or systematic one which would turn up again if we were to repeat the study under similar conditions.

A convention which is often used in this and other tests allows us to omit the word 'positive' when referring to 'positive correlation', and the word 'statistically' when referring to 'statistically significant'.

An important point to remember is that a significant correlation does not by itself tell us anything about causation. If A and B are correlated, it may be that A causes B, that B causes A, that C causes both A and B, or some more complex relation may obtain.

Further Reading

Many of the articles referred to have been reprinted in one or other of the following two books of readings:

Price-Williams, D. R. (1969) *Cross-cultural studies*. Harmondsworth: Penguin.
Berry, J. W. and Dasen, P. R. (1973) *Culture and cognition: readings in cross-cultural psychology*. London: Methuen.

The main journals covering cross-cultural psychology are as follows:

Journal of Social Psychology (founded in 1929, this journal adopted a policy of special consideration for cross-cultural research in 1957).
International Journal of Psychology (started in 1966)
Journal of Cross-cultural Psychology (started in 1970)

The following books treat limited aspects of cross-cultural psychology:

Bruner, J. S., Olver, R. R. and Greenfield, P. M. (1966) *Studies in cognitive growth*. New York: Wiley.
Cole, M., Gay, J., Glick, J. A. and Sharp, D. W. (1971) *The cultural context of learning*. London: Methuen.
Cole, M. and Scribner, S. (1974) *Culture and thought*. New York: Wiley.
Cronbach, L. J. and Drenth, P. (1972) *Mental tests and cultural adaptation*. Hague: Mouton.
Levine, R. A. (1973) *Culture, behaviour and personality*. Chicago: Aldine.

Lloyd, B. B. (1972) *Perception and cognition: a cross-cultural perspective.* Harmondsworth: Penguin

Segall, M. H., Campbell, D. T. and Herskovitz, M. J. (1966) *The influence of culture on visual perception.* New York: Bobbs-Merrill.

Vernon, P. E. (1969) *Intelligence and cultural environment* London: Methuen.

References and Name Index

The numbers in italics following each entry refer to page numbers within this book.

Allport, G. W. and Pettigrew, T. F. (1957) Cultural Influence on the perception of movement: the trapezoidal illusion among Zulus. *Journal of Abnormal and Social Psychology 55*: 104–13. *95*

Angelini, A. L. (1966) Measuring the achievement motive in Brazil. *Journal of Social Psychology 68*: 35–40. *30*

Appelle, S. (1972) Perception and discrimination as a function of orientation: The 'oblique effect' in man and animals. *Psychological Bulletin 78*: 266–78. *105*

Asch, S. E. (1955) Opinions and social pressure. *Scientific American 192*: 31–5. *37*

Ball, J. S. and Byrnes, F. C. (1960) *Research, Principles and Practice in Visual Communication.* Washington, D.C. National Education Association. *107*

Bartlett, F. C. (1932) *Remembering.* Cambridge: University Press. *79*

Bartlett, F. C. (1937) Psychological methods and anthropological problems. *Africa 10*: 401–19. *114*

Benedict, R. (1934) *Patterns of Culture.* Boston, Mass.: Houghton Mifflin. *23*

Berger, P. L., Berger, B. and Kellner, H. (1973) *The Homeless Mind.* New York: Random House. *31, 32*

Berko, J. and Brown, R. (1960) Psycholinguistic research methods. In P. H. Mussen (ed.) *Handbook of Research Methods in Child Development.* New York: Wiley. *107*

Bernstein, B. (1960) Language and social class. *British Journal of Sociology 2*: 217–76. *64*

Berrien, F. K. (1967) Methodological and related problems in cross-cultural research. *International Journal of Psychology 2*: 33–44. *114, 116, 117*

Berry, J. W. (1966) Temne and Eskimo perceptual skills. *International Journal of Psychology 1*: 207–29. *43, 46, 47*

Berry, J. W. (1969) On cross-cultural comparability. *International Journal of Psychology 4*: 119–28. *116*

Berry, J. W. (1971) Ecological and cultural factors in spatial perceptual development. *Canadian Journal of Behavioural Science 3*: 324–36. *46*

Berry, J. W. (1973) Radical cultural relativism and the concept of intelligence. In J. W. Berry and P. R. Dasen (eds) *Culture and Cognition: Readings in Cross-cultural Psychology*. London: Methuen. *118*

Beveridge, W. M. (1935) Racial differences in phenomenal regression. *British Journal of Psychology 26*: 59–62. *97*

Beveridge, W. M. (1939) Some racial differences in perception. *British Journal of Psychology 30*: 57–64. *51*

Biesheuvel, S. (1943) *African Intelligence*. Johannesburg: South African Institute of Personnel Relations. *92*

Bingham, M. G. (1968) The interpretation of diagrams. *Science Education News 4*: 2–4. Zambia Association for Science Education. *110*

Blum, D. M. and Chagnon, J. G. (1967) The effect of age, sex and language on rotation in a visual-motor task. *Journal of Social Psychology 71*: 125–32. *105*

Boas, F. (1927) *Primitive Art*. Oslo: Institute for Sammenlignende Kulturforskning. *110*

Bovet, M. (1973) Cognitive processes among illiterate children and adults. In J. W. Berry and P. R. Dasen (eds) *Culture and Cognition*, Ch. 19. London: Methuen. *73, 78*

Bowman, W. J. (1968) *Graphic Communication*. New York: Wiley. *107*

Braine, L. G. (1973) Perceiving and copying the orientation of geometric shapes. *Journal of Research and Development in Education 6*: 44–55. *105*

Brislin, R. W. (1974) The Ponzo illusion: additional cues, age, orientation. *Journal of Cross-Cultural Psychology, 5* 139–61. *96*

Bruner, J. S. (1966) An overview. In J. S. Bruner, R. R. Olver and P. M. Greenfield (eds) *Studies in Cognitive Growth*, Ch. 14. New York: Wiley. *77, 86*

Bruner, J. S. and Minturn, L. (1955) Perceptual identification and perceptual organization. *Journal of General Psychology 53*: 21–8. *60*

Bryant, P. E. (1974) *Perception and Understanding in Young Children*. London: Methuen. *78, 91, 104*

Buros, O. (1970) *Personality: Tests and Reviews*. New Jersey: Gryphon Press. *27*

126

Campbell, D. T. (1961) The mutual methodological relevance of anthropology and psychology. In F. L. K. Hsu (ed.) *Psychological Anthropology*, pp. 333–52. Homewood, Ill.: Dorsey Press. *74, 117*

Campbell, D. T. (1964) Distinguishing differences of perception from failures of communication in cross-cultural studies. In F. S. C. Northrop and H. H. Livingston (eds) *Cross-cultural Understanding: Epistemology in Anthropology*, Ch. 18. New York: Harper & Row. *116*

Carmichael, L., Hogan, H. P. and Walter, A. A. (1932) An experimental study of the effect of language on the reproduction of visually perceived form. *Journal of Experimental Psychology 15*: 73–86. *60*

Carroll, J. B. and Casagrande, J. B. (1958) The function of language classification in behaviour. In E. E. Maccoby *et al.* (eds) *Readings in Social Psychology*, 27–31 (3rd edn). New York: Holt, Rinehart and Winston. *60*

Chandra, S. (1973) The effects of group pressure in perception: a cross-cultural conformity study in Fiji. *International Journal of Psychology 8*: 37–9. *37*

Child, I. L. (1968) Personality in culture. In E. F. Borgatta and W. W. Lambert (eds) *Handbook of Personality Theory and Research*. Chicago, Ill.: Rand McNally. *21*

Clawson, A. (1962) *The Bender Visual Motor Gestalt Test for Children – A Manual.* California: Western Psychological Services. *94*

Cole, M. and Bruner, J. S. (1971) Cultural differences and inferences about psychological processes. *American Psychologist 26*: 867–76. *71, 86, 111, 118*

Cole, M., Gay, J. Glick, J. A. and Sharp, D. W. (1971) *The Cultural Context of Learning.* London: Methuen. *70, 71, 80, 82, 83, 116*

Cole, M. and Scribner, S. (1974) *Culture and Thought.* New York: Wiley. *81, 85, 96, 97*

Colman, A. M. (1972) 'Scientific' racism and the evidence on race and intelligence. *Race 14*: 132–53. *52*

Conrad, R. (1964) Acoustic confusions in immediate memory. *British Journal of Psychology 55*: 75–84. *60*

Corballis, M. C. and Beale, I. L. (1970) Bilateral symmetry and behaviour. *Psychological Review 77*: 451–61. *104*

Cowley, J. J. and Murray, M. (1962) Some aspects of the development of spatial concepts in Zulu children. *Journal of Social Research, Pretoria 13*: 1–18. *74*

Cronbach, L. J. and Drenth, P. (1972) *Mental tests and Cultural Adaptation.* Hague: Mouton. *119*

Dasen, P. R. (1972) Cross-cultural Piagetian research: a summary. *Journal of Cross-cultural Psychology 3*: 23–40. *69, 72*

Dasen, P. R. (1973) The influence of ecology, culture and European contact on cognitive development in Australian

Aborigines. In J. W. Berry and P. R. Dasen (eds) *Culture and Cognition*, Ch. 24. London: Methuen. *76*

Davidson, H. P. (1935) A study of the confusing letters B, D, P and Q. *Journal of Genetic Psychology* 47: 458–68. *104*

Dawson, J. L. (1967) Cultural and physiological influence upon spatial – perceptual processes in West Africa: Part I. *International Journal of Psychology* 2: 115–28. *43, 45, 46, 52, 106*

Dawson, J. L. M., Young, B. M. and Choi, P. P. C. (1974) Developmental influences in pictorial depth perception among Hong Kong Chinese children. *Journal of Cross-cultural Psychology* 5: 3–22. *104*

De Lemos, M. M. (1973) The development of spatial concepts in Zulu children. In J. W. Berry and P. R. Dasen (eds) *Culture and Cognition*, Ch. 23. London: Methuen. *70, 74*

Deregowski, J. B. (1968a) Difficulties in pictorial depth perception in Africa. *British Journal of Psychology* 59: 195–204. *70, 92, 100, 101, 102*

Deregowski, J. B. (1968b) Pictorial recognition in subjects from a relatively pictureless environment. *African Social Research* 5: 356–64. *99*

Deregowski, J. B. (1969a) Perception of the two- and three-pronged trident by two- and three-dimensional perceivers. *Journal of Experimental Psychology* 82: 9–13. *92*

Deregowski, J. B. (1969b) Preference for chain-type drawings in Zambian domestic servants and primary school children. *Psychologia Africana* 12: 172–80. *108*

Deregowski, J. B. (1970) A note on the possible determinants of split representation as an artistic style. *International Journal of Psychology* 5: 21–6. *108*

Deregowski, J. B. (1972) Reproduction of orientation of Koh-type figures: a cross-cultural study. *British Journal of Psychology* 63: 283–96. *104*

Deregowski, J. B. (1974) Teaching African children pictorial depth perception: in search of a method. *Perception* 3: 309–12. *107*

Deregowski, J. B., Muldrow, E. S. and Muldrow, W. F. (1972) Pictorial recognition in a remote Ethiopian population. *Perception* 1: 417–25. *98*

Deregowski, J. B. and Serpell, R. (1971) Performance on a sorting task: a cross-cultural experiment. *International Journal of Psychology* 6: 273–81. *79*

Descoeudres, A. (1914) Couleur, forme ou nombre? *Archives de Psychologie* 14: 305–41. *60*

Donaldson, M. and Wales, R. J. (1970) On the acquisition of some relational terms. In J. R. Hayes (ed.) *Cognition and the Development of Language*, 235–68. New York: Wiley. *91.*

Duncan, H. F., Gourlay, N. and Hudson, W. (1973) *A Study of Pictorial Perception among Bantu and White Primary School*

Children in South Africa. Johannesburg: Witwatersrand University Press. *89, 92, 106, 108, 109*

Eibl-Eibesfeldt, I. (1970) *Ethology: The Biology of Behaviour.* Translated by E. Klinghammer. New York: Holt, Rinehart & Winston. *15*

Evans, J. L. and Segall, M. H. (1969) Learning to classify by colour and by function: a study of concept-discovery by Ganda children. *Journal of Social Psychology* 77: 35–53. *62*

Faris, J. C. (1972) *Nuba Personal Art.* London: Duckworth. *110*

Farrell, B. A. (1963) Psychoanalysis – II. The method. *New Society* 39 (27 June): 12–14. Reprinted in S. M. C. Lee and M. Herbert (eds) *Freud and Psychology*, Ch. 3. Harmondsworth: Penguin, 1970. *73*

Feather, N. T. and Hutton, M. A. (1974) Value systems of students in Papua New Guinea and Australia. *International Journal of Psychology* 9: 91–104. *32, 33*

Ferguson, C. A. (1959) Diglossia. *Word 15*: 325–40. *63*

Fishman, J. A. (1960) A systematization of the Whorfian hypothesis. *Behavioural Science 5*: 323–39. *55, 59*

Fishman, J. A. (1967) Bilingualism with and without diglossia: diglossia with and without bilingualism. *Journal of Social Issues 23*(2): 29–38. *63*

Flavell, J. H. (1963) *The Developmental Psychology of Jean Piaget.* Princeton, N.J.: Van Nostrand. *69, 75*

Freeman, N. H. (1972) Process and product in children's drawing. *Perception 1*: 123–40. *107*

Frijda, N. and Jahoda, G. (1966) On the scope and methods of cross-cultural research. *International Journal of Psychology 1*: 109–27. *26*

Furby, L. (1971) A theoretical analysis of cross-cultural research in cognitive development: Piaget's conservation task. *Journal of Cross-cultural Psychology 2*: 241–56. *78*

Furth, H. G. (1966) *Thinking without Language. Psychological Implications of Deafness.* New York: Free Press. *58*

Gay, J. and Cole, M. (1967) *The New Mathematics and an Old Culture.* New York: Holt, Rinehart & Winston. *87*

German, G. A. (1972) Aspects of clinical psychiatry in sub-Saharan Africa. *British Journal of Psychiatry 121*: 461–79. *34, 35*

Ghent, L. (1961) Form and its orientation: a child's eye view. *American Journal of Psychology 74*: 177–90. *105*

Ghent, L. (1965) Perception of overlapping and embedded figures by children of different ages. *American Journal of Psychology 69*: 575–87. *48*

Gibson, E. J. and Walk, R. D. (1960) The visual cliff. *Scientific American 202*: 64–71. *98*

Gibson, E. J., Gibson, J. J., Pick, A. D. and Osser, H. (1962) A developmental study of the discrimination of letter-like forms. *Journal of Comparative and Physiological Psychology* 55: 897–906. *104*

Gibson, J. J. (1950) *Perception of the Visual World*. Boston, Mass.: Houghton Mifflin. *102*

Gibson, J. J. (1966) *The Senses Considered as Perceptual Systems*. Boston, Mass.: Houghton Mifflin. *49*

Goffman, E. (1961) *Encounters: Two Studies of the Sociology of Interaction*. Indianapolis, Ia: Bobbs-Merrill. *23*

Goffman, E. (1967) *Interaction Ritual: Essays on Face-to-face Behaviour*. New York: Anchor Doubleday. *24*

Goldstein, K. and Scheerer, M. (1941) Abstract and concrete behaviour; an experimental study with special tests. *Psychological Monographs 53*(2), No. 239. *43, 67*

Gollin, E. S. (1965) Factors affecting conditional discrimination in children. *Journal of Comparative and Physiological Psychology 60*: 422–7. *83*

Gombrich, E. H. (1960) *Art and Illusion*. London: Phaidon. *101, 103, 108, 109, 110, 117*

Goodnow, J. J. (1962) A test of milieu differences with some of Piaget's tasks. *Psychological Monographs 76*: (36) No. 555. *72*

Goodnow, J. J. (1969) Cultural variations in cognitive skills. In D. R. Price-Williams (ed.) *Cross-cultural Studies*, Ch. 14. Harmondsworth: Penguin. *74*

Goodnow, J. J. and Levine, R. A. (1973) The grammar of action: sequence and syntax in children's copying. *Cognitive Psychology 4*: 82–98. *107*

Gottschaldt, K. (1926) The influence of past experience on the perception of figures. *Psychologische Forschung 8*: 261–317. Translated and reproduced in part in M. D. Vernon (ed.) *Experiments in Perception*, Ch. 2. Harmondsworth: Penguin, 1966. *43*

Greenberg, J. M. (ed.) 1963 *Universals of Language*. Cambridge, Mass.: M.I.T. Press. *56*

Greenfield, P. M. (1966) On culture and conservation. In J. S. Bruner, R. R. Olver and P. M. Greenfield *et al.* (eds) *Studies in Cognitive Growth*, Ch. 11. New York: Wiley. *67, 77, 117*

Greenfield, P. M. (1968) Oral or written language: the consequences for cognitive development in Africa and the United States. Paper presented at a *symposium on cross-cultural studies*, American Educational Association, Chicago, Ill., February 1968. *66, 67*

Greenfield, P. M. Reich, L. C. and Olver, R. R. (1966) On culture and equivalence: II. In J. S. Bruner, R. R. Olver and P. M. Greenfield *et al.* (eds) *Studies in Cognitive Growth*, Ch. 13. New York: Wiley. *62, 66*

Gregory, R. L. (1970) *The Intelligent Eye*. London: Weidenfeld & Nicolson. *94, 102*

Gumperz, J. J. and Blom, J. P. (1971) Social meaning in

linguistic structures: code-switching in Norway. In J. J. Gumperz, *Language in Social Groups* (selected and introduced by A. S. Dil), Ch. 16. Stanford, Calif.: University Press. *65*

Gumperz, J. J. and Hernandez, E. (1971) Bilingualism, bi-dialectalism and classroom interaction. In J. J. Gumperz, *op. cit.*, Ch. 17. *65*

Harlow, H. F. (1959) Learning set and error factor theory. In S. Koch (ed.) *Psychology: A Study of a Science, Vol. 5*, 492–537. New York: McGraw-Hill. *82*

Harris, D. B. (1963) *Children's Drawings as Measures of Intellectual Maturity. A Revision and Extension of the Goodenough Draw-a-man Test.* New York: Harcourt, Brace and World. *94*

Held, R. (1965) Plasticity in sensory-motor systems. *Scientific American 213*: 84–94. *106*

Heron, A. and Simonsson, M. (1969) Weight conservation in Zambian children: a non-verbal approach. *International Journal of Psychology* 4: 281–92. *67*

Herriot, P. (1973) Assumptions underlying the use of psychological models in subnormality research. In A. D. B. Clarke and A. M. Clarke (eds) *Mental Retardation and Behavioural Research.* Edinburgh: Churchill Livingstone. *81*

Herskovitz, M. (1959) Art and value. In R. Redfield, M. J. Herskovitz and G. F. Ekholm (eds) *Aspects of Primitive Art*, 42–97. New York: Museum of Primitive Art. *98*

Hockett, C. F. (1964) Scheduling. In F. S. C. Northrop and H. H. Livingston (eds) *Cross-cultural Understanding: Epistemology in Anthropology*, Ch. 8. New York: Harper & Row. *115*

Hoijer, H. (1945) Classificatory verb stems in the Apachean languages. *International Journal of American Linguistics 11*: 13. *60*

Hopkins, B. and Wober, M. (1973) Games and sports: missing items in cross-cultural psychology. *International Journal of Psychology* 8: 5–14. *114*

Howard, I. P. and Templeton, W. B. (1966) *Human Spatial Orientation.* New York: Wiley. *107*

Huang, I. (1945) Abstraction of form and color in children as a function of the stimulus objects. *Journal of Genetic Psychology* 66: 59–62. *60*

Hudson, W. (1960) Pictorial depth perception in sub-cultural groups in Africa. *Journal of Social Psychology 52*: 183–208. *89, 90, 91, 92, 100, 101, 102, 103*

Hudson, W. (1962) Pictorial perception and educational adaptation in Africa. *Psychologie Africana 9*: 226–39. *108*

Hudson, W. (1967) The study of the problem of pictorial perception among unacculturated groups. *International Journal of Psychology 2*: 89–107. *88, 108*

Hunter, I. M. L. (1964) *Memory.* Harmondsworth: Penguin (revised edn). *80*

131

Hyde, D. M. G. (1970) *Piaget and Conceptual Development*. New York: Holt, Rinehart and Winston. *72, 76*

Inhelder, B., Bovet, M., Sinclair, H. and Smock, C. D. (1966) On cognitive development. *American Psychologist 21*: 160–4. *69, 84*

Inkeles, A. (1966) The modernization of man. In M. Weiner (ed.) *Modernization*. New York: Basic Books. *31*

Inkeles, A. and Levinson, D. J. (1969) National character: the study of modal personality and sociocultural systems. In G. Lindzey and E. Aronson (eds) *Handbook of Social Psychology* (2nd edn) vol. 4, 418–506. Cambridge, Mass.: Addison Wesley. *21, 22*

Irwin, M. H., Schafer, G. N. and Feiden, C. P. (1974) Emic and unfamiliar category sorting of Mano farmers and U.S. undergraduates. *Journal of Cross-cultural Psychology 5*: 407–23. *62, 113*

Jahoda, G. (1966) Geometric illusions and environment: a study in Ghana. *British Journal of Psychology 57*: 193–9. *96*

Jahoda, G. (1970) Supernatural beliefs and changing cognitive structures among Ghanaian University students. *Journal of Cross-Cultural Psychology 1*: 115–30. *33*

Jahoda, G. (in press) Reproduction of Kohs-type figures by Ghanaian children: orientation error revisited. *British Journal of Psychology*. *106*

Jeffrey, W. E. (1968) The orienting reflex and attention in cognitive development. *Psychological Review 75*: 323–34. *83*

Jensen, A. R. (1970) A two-level theory of mental abilities. In A. R. Jensen and W. D. Rohwer (eds) *An Experimental Analysis of Learning Abilities in Culturally Disadvantaged Children*. Final Report: Office of Economic Opportunity, Contract No. OEO 2404: cyclostyled. *80*

Jensen, A. R. and Frederiksen, J. (1970) Social class differences in free recall of categorised and uncategorised lists. In A. R. Jensen and W. D. Rohwer (eds) *op. cit*. *80*

Kavadias, G. (1966) The assimilation of the scientific and technological 'message'. *International Social Science Journal 18*: 362–75. *33*

Kellaghan, T. D. (1968) Abstraction and categorization in African children. *International Journal of Psychology 3*: 115–20. *62*

Kendler, H. H. and Kendler, T. S. (1962) Vertical and horizontal processes in problem solving. *Psychological Review 69*: 1–16. *58, 82*

Kernan, C. M. (1972) Language behaviour in a black urban community. *Monographs of the Language-Behaviour Research Laboratory*, No. 2. University of California. *65*

Kilbride, P. L., Robbins, M. C. and Freeman, R. B. (1968) Pictorial depth perception and education among Baganda school children. *Perceptual and Motor Skills 26*: 1116–18. *101*

Kingsley, P. R. (1974) The development by Zambian children of strategies for doing intellectual work. *H.D.R.U. Reports 24*. University of Zambia: cyclostyled. *85–6*

Kingsley, P. R., Allison, O. and Noble, M. (n.d.) Pictorial depth perception as a function of 'symbolic' versus 'realistic' pictorial material (unpublished MS). *91, 103*

Kunkel, J. (1970) *Society and Economic Growth*. New York: Oxford University Press. *31*

Labov, W. (1969) The logic of non-standard English. *Georgetown Monographs on Language and Linguistics, 22*. *68*

Leighton, A. H., Lambo, T. A., Hughes, C. C., Leighton, D. C., Murphy, J. M. and Macklin, D. B. (1963) *Psychiatric Disorder among the Yoruba*. New York: Cornell University Press. *34*

Lemon, N. (1973) Linguistic development and personal constructs: some implications for language policy in education. Paper presented at the African Regional Conference of the *International Association for Cross-cultural Psychology*. Ibadan, Nigeria, April 1973. *64*

Lenneberg, E. H. (1967) *Biological Foundations of Language*. New York: Wiley. *15*

Lester, M. (1974) Bilingual education in the United States, the Pacific and South East Asia. In R. W. Brislin (ed.) *Topics in Culture Learning*, Vol. 2, 137–46. Honolulu: East–West Culture Learning Institute. *66*

Levine, R. A. (1966) *Dreams and Deeds: Achievement Motivation in Nigeria*. Chicago, Ill.: University Press. *28*

Levine, R. A. (1973) *Culture, Behaviour and Personality*. Chicago, Ill.: Aldine. *21, 24, 28*

Lévi-Strauss, C. (1963) *Structural Anthropology*. New York: Basic Books (*Anthropologie Structurale*, originally published Paris, 1958). *86, 108*

Luria, A. R. (1961) *The Role of Speech in the Regulation of Normal and Abnormal Behaviour*. London: Pergamon Press. *58*

McClelland, D. C. (1961) *The Achieving Society*. Princeton, N.J.: Van Nostrand. *28, 29, 30*

McClelland, D. C., Atkinson, J. W., Clark, R. A. and Lowell, E. L. (1953) *The Achievement Motive*. New York: Appleton-Century-Crofts. *29*

McFie, J. (1961) The effect of education on African performance on a group of intellectual tests. *British Journal of Educational Psychology 31*: 232–40. *104*

McLuhan, M. (1962) *The Gutenberg Galaxy*. London: Routledge & Kegan Paul. *44*

Maclay, H. (1958) An experimental study of language and nonlinguistic behaviour. *Southwestern Journal of Anthropology 14*: 220–9. *62*

MacNamara, J. (1967) Effects of instruction in a weaker language. *Journal of Social Issues 23*(2): 121–35. *66*

Maehr, M. L. (1974) Culture and achievement motivation. *American Psychologist 29*: 887–96. *30*

Maistriaux, R. (1955) La sous-évolution des noirs d'Afrique. Sa nature-ses causes-ses remèdes. *Revue de Psychologie des Peuples 10*: 167–456. *104*

Maslow, A. H. (1954) *Motivation and Personality*. New York: Harper. *32*

Masserman, J. H. (1943) *Behaviour and Neurosis*. Chicago, Ill.: University Press. *37*

Mead, M. (1949) *Male and Female: A Study of the Sexes in a Changing World*. New York: Morrow. *20*

Miller, G. A. (1956) The magical number seven plus or minus two: some limits on our capacity for processing information. *Psychological Review 63*: 81–97. *79*

Miller, R. J. (1973) Cross-cultural research in the perception of pictorial materials. *Psychological Bulletin 80*: 135–50. *89, 99*

Mkilifi, M. H. A. (1972) Triglossia and Swahili–English bilingualism in Tanzania. *Language in Society 1*: 197–213. *65*

Moody, J. (1973) Possible sources of error in the English of first-year students at the University of Zambia: some implications for the teaching of English in Zambia. *Bulletin of the Zambian Language Group 1*(2): 67–82. *64*

Morris, J. B. (1967) The rod-and-frame box: a portable version of the rod-and-frame test. *Perceptual and Motor Skills 25*: 152. *51*

Mundy-Castle, A. C. (1966) Pictorial depth perception in Ghanaian children. *International Journal of Psychology 1*: 290–300. *91, 101*

Mundy-Castle, A. C. and Nelson, G. K. (1962) A neuropsychological study of the Knysna forest workers. *Psychologia Africana 9*: 240–72. *92, 97*

Munroe, R. L., Munroe, R. H. and Daniels, R. E. (1969) Effects of status and values on estimation of coin size in two East African communities. *Journal of Social Psychology 77*: 25–34. *37*

Murray, M. M. (1961) *The development of spatial concepts in African and European children*. Unpublished M.Sc. thesis, University of Natal. *74*

Okonji, M. O. (1969) The differential effects of rural and urban upbringing on the development of cognitive styles. *International Journal of Psychology 4*: 293–305. *42, 43, 46, 47*

Okonji. M. O. (1971) A cross-cultural study of the effects of familiarity on classificatory behaviour. *Journal of Cross-cultural Psychology 2*: 39–50. *49, 78*

Okonji, M. O. (1972) *Child rearing and the development of cognitive style in Uganda*. University of Zambia: cyclostyled. *38, 42, 47*

Olson, D. R. (1970) Language and thought: *Psychological Review* 77: 257–73. *90*

Omari, I. M. and Cook, H. (1972) Differential cognitive cues in pictorial depth perception. *Journal of Cross-Cultural Psychology* 3: 321–5. *91*

Orley, J. H. (1970) *Culture and Mental Illness*. Kampala: Makerere Institute of Social Research. *34*

Over, R. (1968) Explanations of geometrical illusions. *Psychological Bulletin 70*: 545–62. *96*

Page, H. W. (1970) Pictorial depth perception: a note. *South African Journal of Psychology 1*: 45–8. *91*

Parkin, D. J. (1974) Language switching in Nairobi. In W. H. Whiteley (ed.) *Language in Kenya*, Ch. 8. Oxford: University Press. *65*

Piaget, J. (1954) Le Langage et la Pensée du point de vue génétique. *Acta Psychologica, Amsterdam 10*: 51–60. *58*

Piaget, J. and Inhelder, B. (1956) *The Child's Conception of Space*. London: Routledge & Kegan Paul. *91*

Poortinga, Y. H. (1971) Cross-cultural comparison of maximum performance tests: some methodological aspects and some experiments with simple auditory and visual stimuli. *Psychologia Africana, Monograph Supplement No. 6. 93*

Potter, M. C. (1966) On perceptual recognition. In J. S. Bruner, R. C. Olver and P. M. Greenfield *et al.* (eds) *Studies in Cognitive Growth*. New York: Wiley. *99*

Price-Williams, D. R. (1961) A study concerning concepts of conservation of quantities among primitive children. *Acta Psychologica 19*: 669–70. *72*

Price-Williams, D. R. (1962) Abstract and concrete modes of classification in a primitive society. *British Journal of Educational Psychology 32*: 50–61. *79*

Price-Williams, D., Gordon, W. and Ramirez, M. (1969) Skill and conservation. *Developmental Psychology 1*: 769. *76*

Prince, J. R. (1968) The effect of Western education on science conceptualisation in New Guinea. *British Journal of Educational Psychology 38*: 64–74. *77*

Reuter, E. B. (1941) *Handbook of Sociology*. New York: Dryden. *20*

Rivers, W. H. R. (1901) Vision. In A. C. Haddon (ed.) *Reports of the Cambridge Anthropological Expedition to the Torres Straits*, vol. 2, Pt. 1. Cambridge: University Press. *95*

Rudel, R. G. and Teuber, H.-L. (1963) Discrimination of line in children. *Journa of Comparative and Physiological Psychology 56*: 892–8. *104*

Sapir, E. (1929) The status of linguistics as a science. *Language 5*: 207–14. *58*

Segall, M. H., Campbell, D. T. and Herskovits, M. J. (1966) *The Influence of Culture on Visual Perception*. New York: Bobbs-Merrill. *95, 96, 113*

Serpell, R. (1966) Selective attention in matching form by children. *H.R.D.U. Reports 2.* University of Zambia: cyclostyled. *60*

Serpell, R. (1968) Selective attention and interference between first and second languages. *University of Zambia, Institute for Social Research Communication 4* (monograph). *64*

Serpell, R. (1969a) Cultural differences in attentional preference for colour over form. *International Journal of Psychology 4*: 1–8. *62*

Serpell, R. (1969b) The influence of language, education and culture on attentional preference between colour and form. *International Journal of Psychology 4*: 183–94. *62*

Serpell, R. (1971a) Discrimination of orientation by Zambian children. *Journal of Comparative and Physiological Psychology 75*: 312–16. *104*

Serpell, R. (1971b) Preference for specific orientation of abstract shapes among Zambian children. *Journal of Cross-cultural Psychology 2*: 225–39. *105*

Serpell, R. (1973) Applications of attention theory to teaching in schools for the severely subnormal. In A. D. B. Clarke and A. M. Clarke (eds) *Mental Retardation and Behavioural Research*, pp. 167–80. Edinburgh and London: Churchill Livingstone. *84*

Serpell, R. (1974) Aspects of intelligence in a developing country. *African Social Research 17*: 578–96. *49, 93, 113*

Serpell, R. and Deregowski, J. B. (1972) Teaching pictorial depth perception: a classroom study. *H.D.R.U. Reports 21*: University of Zambia: cyclostyled. *107*

Shapiro, M. B. (1960) The rotation of drawings by illiterate Africans. *Journal of Social Psychology 52*: 17–30. *104*

Sharma, R. (1973) The reading skills of Grade Three children. *Psychological Service Reports 1/1973*. Lusaka: Ministry of Education and Culture. *64*

Sherman, J. A. (1967) Problems of sex differences in space perception and aspects of intellectual functioning. *Psychological Review 74*: 290–9. *43*

Siann, G. (1972) Measuring field dependence in Zambia. *International Journal of Psychology 7*: 87–96. *43, 45, 48, 54*

Sigel, I., Anderson, L. M. and Shapiro, H. (1966) Categorization behaviour of lower and middle class negro pre-school children: differences in dealing with representation of familiar objects. *Journal of Negro Education 35*: 218–29. *79*

Slamecka, N. J. (1968) A methodological analysis of shift paradigms in human discrimination learning. *Psychological Bulletin 69*: 423–38. *83*

Slobin, D. I. (1968) Questions of language development in cross-cultural perspective. *Paper Presented at Symposium on Language Learning in Cross-cultural Perspective*. Michigan, September 1968. *64*

Spock, B. M. (1970) *Baby and Child Care*. New York: Pocket Books. *40*

Stevenson, H. W., Iscoe, I. and McConnell, C. (1955) A developmental study of transposition. *Journal of Experimental Psychology 49*: 278–80. *84*

Stewart, V. M. (1973) Tests of the 'carpentered world' hypothesis by race and environment in America and Zambia. *International Journal of Psychology 8*: 83–94. *95*

Stewart, V. M. (1974) A cross-cultural test of the 'carpentered world' hypothesis using the Ames distorted room illusion. *International Journal of Psychology 9*: 79–90. *95*

Strangman, E. (1967) *Achievement in Fantasy: a Study of Achievement Imagery in the TAT Stories and Dream Reports of American Adolescents*. Unpublished Ph.D. dissertation, University of Chicago. *28*

Suchmann, R. G. (1966) Cultural differences in children's color and form preferences. *Journal of Social Psychology 70*: 3–10. *62*

Sumotirto, B. W. (1962) Social attitudes among high school students in Indonesia. *British Journal of Educational Psychology 32*: 3–11. *32*

Tajfel, H. (1957) Value and the perceptual judgement of magnitude. *Psychological Review 64*: 192–204. *37*

Tajfel, H. (1969) Social and cultural factors in perception. In G. Lindzey and E. Aronson (eds) *Handbook of Social Psychology, Vol. 3*, Ch. 22. Reading, Mass.: Addison Wesley. *117*

Thouless, R. H. (1932) A racial difference in perception. *Journal of Social Psychology 4*: 330–9. *97*

Trabasso, T., Deutsch, J. A. and Gelman, R. (1966) Attention and discrimination learning of young children. *Journal of Experimental Child Psychology 4*: 9–19. *83, 84*

Turnbull, C. (1961) *The Forest People: A Study of Pygmies of the Congo*. New York: Simon & Schuster. *97*

Unzapass (University of Zambia Student Psychological Association) (1972) Formation of close friendships among Zambian University students. University of Zambia: unpublished MS. *65*

Vernon, M. D. (1970) *Perception through Experience*. London: Methuen. *97, 98*

Vernon, P. E. (1964) *Personality Assessment: A Critical Survey*. London: Methuen. *27*

Vernon, P. E. (1969) *Intelligence and Cultural Environment*. London: Methuen. *119*

Watson, J. B. (1925) *Behaviourism*. New York: Norton. *10*

Weaver, D. B. (1974) *An Intra-cultural Test of Empiricistic vs. Physiological Explanations for Cross-cultural Differences in Geometric Illusion Susceptibility Using Two Illusions in Ghana*. Unpublished doctoral dissertation, Northwestern University, Evanston, Illinois. *96*

Wechsler, D. (1944) *The Measurement of Adult Intelligence*. Baltimore: Williams and Wilkins. *119*

Welford, A. J. (1968) *Fundamentals of Skill*. London: Methuen. *87*

Werner, H. (1940) *Comparative Psychology of Mental Development*. New York: Science Editions. *108*

Whiting. B. B. (ed.) (1963) *Six Cultures: Studies of Child-rearing*. New York: Wiley. *25*

Whiting, J. W. M. and Child, I. L. (1953) *Child Training and Personality: A Cross-cultural Study*. New Haven: Conn.: Yale University Press. *25, 28*

Whittaker, J. O. and Meade, R. D. (1967) Social pressure in the modification and distortion of judgement: a cross-cultural study. *International Journal of Psychology* 2: 109–13. *37*

Whorf, B. L. (1956) *Language, Thought and Reality: Selected Writings of Benjamin Lee Whorf* (edited by J. B. Carroll). New York: Wiley. *58, 59, 70*

Witkin, H. A. (1959) The perception of the Upright. *Scientific American* 200: 50–6. *37, 38, 40, 51*

Witkin, H. A. (1967) A cognitive style approach to cross-cultural research. *International Journal of Psychology* 2: 233–50. *40*

Witkin, H. A. and Asch, S. E. (1948) Studies in space orientation – IV. Further experiments on perception of the upright with displaced visual fields. *Journal of Experimental Psychology* 38: 762–82. *50*

Witkin, H. A., Dyk, R. B., Faterson, H. F., Goodenough, D. R. and Karp, S. A. (1962) *Psychological Differentiation: Studies of Development*. New York: Wiley. *42, 51*

Witkin, H. A., Goodenough, D. R. and Karp, S. A. (1967) Stability of cognitive style from childhood to young adulthood. *Journal of Personality and Social Psychology* 7: 291–300. *42, 51*

Witkin, H. A., Price-Williams, D. R., Bertini, M., Christiansen, B., Oltman, P. K., Ramirez, M. and Van Meel, J. (1974) Social conformity and psychological differentiation. *International Journal of Psychology* 9: 11–30. *51, 54*

Wittgenstein, L. (1958) *Philosophical Investigations* (translated by G. E. M. Anscombe). Oxford: Blackwell (2nd edn). *90*

Wober, M. (1966) Sensotypes. *Journal of Social Psychology* 70: 181–9. *42, 43, 44, 89, 92*

Wober, M. (1967) Adapting Witkin's field independence theory to accommodate new information from Africa. *British Journal of Psychology* 58: 29–38. *42, 43, 44, 49, 50, 52, 53*

Wober, M. (1969) Distinguishing centri-cultural from cross-cultural tests and research. *Perceptual and Motor Skills* 28: 488. *54, 113*

Wober, M. and Bukombi, S. (1973) The shifty risk phenomenon and changing attitudes to birth control in Uganda. *Occasional*

Paper No. 20. Sociology Dept., Makerere University, Kampala. *31*

Wohlwill, J. F. (1965) Texture of the stimulus field and age as variables in the perception of relative distance. *Journal of Experimental Child Psychology 2*: 163–77. *103*

Wolff, J. L. (1967) Concept-shift and discrimination-reversal learning in humans. *Psychological Bulletin 68*: 369–408. *83*

Yates, A. J. (1956) The rotation of drawings by brain-damaged patients. *Journal of Abnormal and Social Psychology 53*: 178–81. *105*